Flippin Good Recipes,

From Flippin Arkansas

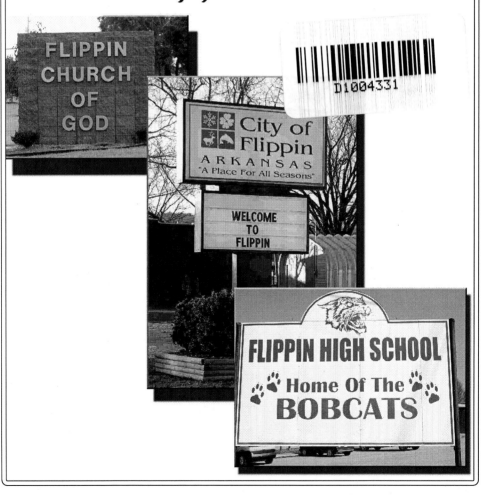

FLIPPIN CHURCH OF GOD

City of Flippin
ARKANSAS
"A Place For All Seasons"

WELCOME TO FLIPPIN

FLIPPIN HIGH SCHOOL
Home Of The BOBCATS

D1004331

Flippin Good Recipes,

From Flippin Arkansas

A collection of wonderful recipes,
family profiles, helpful tips,
photographs of the area and more!
Brought to you by the Flippin Pride Team,
a nonprofit organization.

Copyright 2006 © Whitehall Publishing, Yellville, Arkansas with The Flippin Pride Team, a nonprofit organization located in Flippin, Arkansas

Printed in the U.S.A., Canada and Europe.
All rights reserved. Reproduction in whole or in part without written permission is prohibited.

For more information, visit us on the Web at:

flippinprideteam.org or whitehallpublishing.com

E-mail us at:

flprideteam@flippinweb.com or
info@whitehallpublishing.com

or write to us at:

The Flippin Pride Team
P.O. Box 1191
Flippin, AR 72634 USA

ISBN# 0-9772372-3-0

Dedication

This book is dedicated to all the residents of Flippin Arkansas who share a love of the Ozarks, of Flippin and of the life-style that thrives in this part of the country.

Acknowledgment

The Flippin Pride Team would like to acknowledge and thank Whitehall Publishing, the citizens of the Flippin community, the Flippin newspaper: The Mountaineer Echo, Flippin City Hall, Arvest Bank, U.S. Bank, Pizza Hut and the Baxter Bulletin newspaper.

The Flippin Pride Team

The Flippin Pride Team was founded in 1998 by a handful of Flippin residents who wanted to give-back to their local community where they live, work and play.

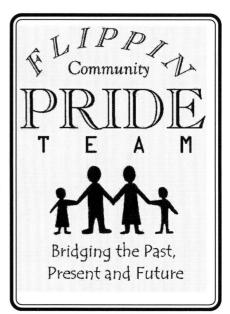

Over the years, the Flippin Pride Team has grown in numbers and in their ability to help the community in a wide variety of ways. The Flippin Pride Team is a nonprofit organization.

The Flippin Pride Team sponsors the following events each year:

* *The Annual Fish Fry & Gospel Sing (May)*
* *The 3rd of July Fireworks Celebration park Festivities*
* *The Holi-Dazzle Parade and Christmas Lighting*

The Club also participates in the Community Wish For Kids program. In 2005, the Flippin Pride Team selected over 35 names of children in need and went on a shopping spree for them at our new Flippin Super Wal-Mart. Afterwards, the group gathered together to wrap each and every gift for the children to make certain that on Christmas morning these children would have a day to remember.

Beyond that, and possibly some of the most important things the Flippin Pride Team does each year is to raise money to award college scholarships and to purchase band instruments for the Flippin School. The club is extremely proud of the Flippin Bobcat Marching Band which is recognized nationally for their talent and skill.

Table of Contents

Introduction

You are going to discover that some of the finest people in the world live right here in Flippin Arkansas, even if they do enjoy a good dish of fried bull frog from time to time! Over the years, Flippin Arkansas has certainly been on the receiving end of more than its fair share of jokes due to our unique name. Feel free to smile at the name, enjoy the recipes and discover why Flippin is referred to as God's Country.

From Squirrel and Dumplings to Chicken Jambalaya, this cook book has it all! From Catfish Cakes to Chocolate Gravy, you are going to find some of the most unusual and funny recipes in the world, right here in the *"Flippin Good Recipes, from Flippin Arkansas cookbook."*

In addition to having some of the finest food in the South and the best people around, we also have some of the best fishing in the world. With the Bull Shoals and Norfolk lakes and the world-famous trout-filled White River all within easy driving distance, Flippin Arkansas is a fisherman's paradise. And, if that wasn't enough to get you to come on down for a visit, Ranger Boats is head quartered right here in Flippin Arkansas! If you could ever get tired of fishing, Branson Missouri is just up the interstate.

Of all the recipes in the book, below is our favorite:

Take a dash of family, mix in a cup of caring, add a pound of hard work, patience and tolerance and sprinkle with a good sense of humor and you have Flippin Arkansas, one of the best places in the country to live, fish and eat.

Due to popular demand, watch for volume 2 later this year and be sure to come on down for a visit!

Flippin, Arkansas
Town History

In the early 1800's land in Arkansas was being homesteaded by adventurers from Tennessee, Kentucky, Georgia and the Carolinas. In 1820 Thomas J. Flippin and several members of the Flippin family left Hopkins County, Kentucky, bound for Arkansas. In 1821 they settled near where the Marion County Airport is now located.

Thomas J. Flippin

As time passed, a town of sorts grew; there was a general store, flour mill and a cotton gin. A traveling salesman called the place Goatville, but early residents called it Flippin Barrens to honor the early settler. Self-reliance and pride were not short among the early residents.

In 1904 the railroad came through fields almost a mile from the town. When a merchant moved his store from the old town to the railroad site, other businesses followed and the 'new town' of Flippin came into existence.

Twenty acres of land were purchased and platted into streets and lots by the Marion County Town Company. A well, with a hand pump, was drilled in the middle of Main Street, and it supplied the homes and businesses with water. The streets were graveled and not very wide and a creek ran through town complete with swinging foot-bridges.

The railroad effected the growth of the community and new businesses included a lumber store, cafe, general store, a telephone company, a bank exchange, and a place to sell poultry, eggs and produce. A hotel operated at Girard and Second Street. Other businesses included a livery barn, blacksmith shops, a clothing store and a small novelty shop. The town had a doctor

Flippin Main Street
early Flippin 1900's

but no dentist or optometrist, and an eye specialist, made regular trips to Flippin by train and set up temporary offices in the hotel.

In the 1920's The Real Art Theatre was a successful operation. The place of worship was the Union Church located where the First Baptist Church now stands and the Assembly of God and the Christian Churches were built.

Old Rose Hotel

By 1921 the town was incorporated and James M. Keeter became the first mayor. Cars began to appear and a service station and repair shop opened between Second and Third on Main Street.

Row crops were a way of life and two cotton gins ran full-blast in the autumn as well as a tomato canning factory. Flippin had lots of good timber and stave mills offered employment cutting staves for whiskey barrels or cutting the bolts to make staves.

The post office and a general store operated at the end of West Main Street. Parnell's store carried a good line of Peters Red Goose shoes and the children always got a whistle or popper if they behaved nicely while getting shoes. Several mercantile businesses thrived offering merchandise ranging from candy to coffins.

At this time school for Flippin children was about one-half mile north of what is now, Highway No. 178. Buses, lunchrooms and hot lunches were unheard of and completely unknown.

During the 1930's and 1940's Flippin, along with the rest of the country coped with the depression and the war. The early 1940's stripped the town of able-bodied young men. Those not in the service went to the cities for employment and to help in the war effort.

Callison's Drug and Sundries store offered groceries, patent medicine, clothing and a good, five-cent ice cream cone. Main Street merchants included: Daffron's Cafe, Irene McCracken's

Cafe, Wood Garage, C & J Lumber Company, A. M. Seawright's Grocery, a gas station, a hardware store, the WNC Theatre, and the first tourist court (motel) in Flippin.

There was no pharmacist and the doctor carried his medicine with him to mix when needed.

Old Wood Garage on Main Street, 1934

During the 1940's, workers came from all over the United States to help build the monstrous Bull Shoals Dam. Businesses thrived and an effort was necessary to keep the peace and slow the traffic in the boom town. Marion County had beer and whiskey but Baxter and Boone counties were dry; so the problems were many.

Over the next 30 years Flippin attracted furniture stores, clothing stores and shoe stores, along with various other businesses. In the 1950's city projects included black-topping the streets and installing a water and fire protection system.

Many early-day Flippin businesses, including a hotel and meat market, suffered devastating fires because the bucket brigades did not afford much of a chance for saving the buildings. In 1957 a fire truck was obtained and a volunteer fire department was organized. The building was purchased which houses the fire station and city hall.

In the 1960's Flippin became a city of the second class after a special census in 1965 put the population at more than 500. Street signs and a sewer system were installed, and in 1967 natural gas became available and was a big help to the residents. In 1968 Ranger Boats was founded by Forrest Wood in Flippin.

Iron Mountain Train Station 1903-1969

The town continued to grow rapidly with new businesses, subdivisions and new industry. The special census in 1975 showed a population of 1026.

Now-a days, fishing and boating highlight Flippin's way of life. Flippin is located in the beautiful Ozark Mountains of north central Arkansas and nearby to the gigantic Bull Shoals Lake, the White River, and Buffalo National River and Park. The area offers scenic beauty, a pleasantly mild climate, and outstanding recreational opportunities.

Flippin has excellent schools, two-year colleges only minutes away, a growing population, and access to high-quality medical care. Flippin has an official city population of 1,357 and employs residents from all of Marion and surrounding counties.

Flippin is the home of Ranger Boats. The well-known Ranger brand bass boat was created and has been built in Flippin since 1968. Additional jobs come from industries which make molded plastic parts and cable technology. The tourism industry offers employment to a considerable number of area residents.

Flippin is growing, perhaps faster than any other town in the county. And, with its growth, ends an era our pioneer forefathers might perhaps mourn, for it ends that age of man combating raw, primitive nature, the thing they faced most in their journey to Arkansas and their struggle to create this town named Flippin.

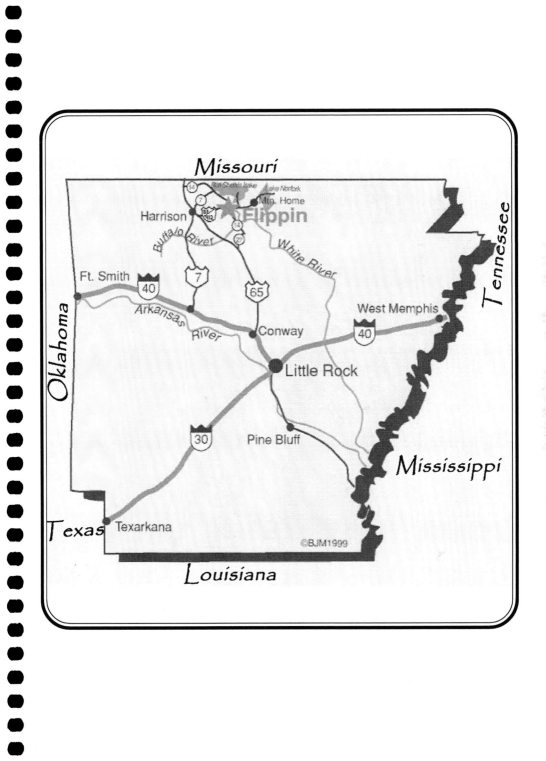

Missouri

Harrison

Flippin

Mtn. Home

Lake Norfork

Buffalo River

White River

Ft. Smith

40

7

65

Arkansas

River

Conway

West Memphis

40

Oklahoma

Little Rock

30

Pine Bluff

Mississippi

Texas

Texarkana

©BJM1999

Tennessee

Louisiana

9

The History of Our Food
and Our Cooks Here in the Ozarks

Sweetnin's

Sweetnin's is a mixture of butter and sorghum. Ozark pioneers made sweetnin's because sugar was so expensive. Sorghum is found throughout the south and has a deep, rich flavor. Sorghum molasses is made from sorghum cane and the word "molasses" actually means "thick, like honey." To make sweetnin's, sorghum and butter are mixed together in a bowl with a fork. Biscuits or bread are then dipped or sopped in the mixture. Sweetnin's was generally served at every meal.

Grits

Hominy grits, or just plain grits, are an institution in the South. The word grits comes from the Old English "grytt", for "bran". In the South, "hominy" came to mean skinned kernels that were ground coarsely to make grits. Many Southerners will tell you the only hominy worth eating is old-fashioned, stone-ground, small hominy, or grits, cooked with water or milk.

Pokeweed

Pokeweed was introduced to our forefathers by the American Indians. Pokeweed is a robust perennial potherb that grows wild in the eastern United States, best known and most cherished in the Deep South.

Pokeweed is a strong smelling herb that can grow to nine feet tall with large, alternate leaves and a poisonous, carrot like tap root. Greenish-white flowers are produced in long clusters, and the flattened berries change from green to shiny purplish-black.

Legendary poke salat (pokeweed) is the best known, most widely consumed wild vegetable in America. For generations, Southerners have plucked the young shoots and leaves of the pokeweed, simmered them in a pot, enjoying their unique, earthy flavor. Check out the "Side Dishes" category for a recipe to make Poke Salat!

Jewell Tilley

Jewell Tilley was born in 1915. He learned to cook at age 15. His worst experiences in the kitchen happened when he cooked food that tasted awful. He once said, "Sometimes it was so bad the dogs wouldn't eat it!" One of Jewell's favorite recipes was baked opossum. To cook an opossum, you place a sweet potato in the belly of the animal, along with a few strips of bacon.

Margie Pauline Duffy

Margie Pauline Duffy grew up in Marion County, Arkansas. Her family made biscuits three times a day, once for every meal and cornbread almost as often. She had a hog killin' grandfather and sixteen hogs were fattened a year to eat. They would cure the ham in the smoke house out back of the home. The only things they bought were coffee, sugar and dried beans. Margie carried her lunch of biscuits and sausage to school in a syrup bucket. A really good fried pie was just sugar, butter and cocoa mixed up in a dough and fried. they used a lot of sorghum and picked nuts. To store food, they would bury cabbage under the hay and dry fruit and pumpkins. No one canned until the 1900's because there were not pressure steamers. Margie's grandmother started canning tomatoes in 1909.

Thelma McCracken

Thelma McCracken grew up in the Peel area of Bull Shoals lake, north of Flippin. Thelma learned to cook at the age of seventeen when her mother died. The first whole turkey she cooked was a disaster when she realized she had forgotten to remove the intestines. Today, those items come in a bag inside the turkey but in Thelma's early days of cooking, they were the real deal!

Weights and Measures

We hope that these charts will help make your time in the kitchen more enjoyable!

Metric Conversions

1 cup	=	250 (ml)
1/4 cup	=	62 1/2 ml
1 teaspoon	=	5 ml
1 tablespoon	=	15 ml
1 pint	=	.47 liter (l)
1 quart	=	.95 liter (l)
1 gallon	=	3.8 liter (l)
1 liter	=	2.1 pints
1 liter	=	1.06 qts
1 liter	=	.26 gallons

Weights and Measures

3 teaspoons	= 1 tbls
4 tablespoons	= 1/4 cup
5 1/2 tablespoons	= 1/3 cup
8 tablespoons	= 1/2 cup
10 2/3 tablespoon	= 2/3 cup
12 tablespoons	= 3/4 cup
16 tablespoons	= 1 cup
1 tablespoon	= 1/2 fluid oz
1 cup	= 8 fluid oz
1 cup	= 1/2 pint
2 cups	= 1 pint
4 cups	= 1 quart
2 pints	= 1 quart
4 quarts	= 1 gallon

Candy Temp Chart

230 - 234 degrees	= Thread
234 - 240 degrees	= Soft Ball
244 - 248 degrees	= Firm Ball
250 - 266 degrees	= Hard Ball
270 - 290 degrees	= Soft Crack
300 - 310 degrees	= Hard Crack

*Above 310 degrees,
your kitchen
is probably on fire!*

Equivalency Chart

1 cup butter or margarine=	1/2 pound
1 cup cheddar cheese =	1/4 pound
1 cup eggs =	4 - 5 whole eggs 8 egg whites or 12 egg yolks
1 cup all-purpose flour =	1/4 pound
1 envelope of gelatin =	1/4 ounce or 1 tbsp
1 cup lard or solid vegetable fat=	1/2 pound
1 medium lemon (juice) =	1 1/2 fluid ounces or 3 tablespoons
1 cup chopped nuts =	1/4 pound

BREADS

"Flowers for Flippin"

In 1956 the Apple Blossom Home Demonstration Club sponsored a flower box contest in a effort to beautify Flippin and encourage pride in the town. All residences and businesses in Flippin were encouraged to participate by displaying a flower box filled with flowers.

Patterned after the successful Neosha, Missouri flower box plan, the contest was embraced by the townspeople of Flippin. Flower boxes were constructed, painted and planted with colorful flowers.

To raise the prize money, letters were sent to local businesses, state political figures and national celebrities asking for contributions. As proof of the good publicity they were bringing to Flippin, crooner Bing Crosby sent a check for $10.00 in prize money and an autographed photo signed "All success in your flower box contest".

"Flowers for Flippin" was a huge success, involving virtually everyone in Flippin. Out of town judges judged the flower boxes and many favorable comments were expressed. Some judges even expressed they wished they lived in Flippin.

The town of Flippin had became known as "The City Of Flowers"!

Flippin Family

The Founding Family

In 1820 Thomas J. Flippin ventured from Hopkins County, Kentucky to Marion County, Arkansas. He and family members settled near an indian grist mill about a mile from where the city of Flippin is located today. To honor the early Flippin family settlers, the townspeople named the growing community Flippin Barrens.

Thomas J. Flippin

History chronicles Thomas J. Flippin serving as a trusted scout during the Revolutionary War transporting war material from Bedford to Fort Patrick Henry. In 1800 he traveled to Monroe County, Kentucky, settling near what became the town of Pikesville and flourished as a well-to-do farmer. Tragically, four of his sons were killed in the War of 1812.

Thomas H. Flippin (son of Thomas J.) lived in Kentucky and Tennessee. He served as a sergeant in the War of 1812 and came by riverboat to Marion County in 1837, settling in Flippin Barrens. Thomas H. served as Clerk of Marion County and was a successful farmer.

Thomas H. P. (Perry) Flippin (son of Thomas H.) married Harriet Tabor, sister of John Tabor, one of the first pioneers of Marion County. Thomas H. P. (Perry) served as Clerk of Marion County.

Judge W. B. Flippin (also son of Thomas H.) served during the Civil War as Captain of a Company, and as Quartermaster of McBride's Brigade. He served Marion County in the House of Representatives. Judge W. B. was well educated and held almost every Marion County office. He was an elder and preacher in the Christian Church. James A. Flippin (son of W. B. Flippin) was a legislator and minister.

The Flippin family represents courage and determination. Today many descendants of the original Flippin founding family, from the 1800's, still reside in Flippin and throughout Marion County.

Flippin Well & Pump

Serving the Flippin Area for Over 100 Years

The Flippin Well & Pump business, originally started by William 'Uncle Bill' McCracken, can trace it's beginnings back to the early 1900's. In the early years, well drilling was done using a steam powered drill.

The drilling business was formerly known as D. R. Moore Well & Drilling. Since 1967 the business has operated as Flippin Bros. Drilling & Pump Service, being owned at that time by brothers Harold and James Flippin.

Marcus Flippin currently owns and operates the business as Flippin Well & Pump. His daughter, Erica Morris, is the 5th generation of the Flippin founding family descendents to work in the business. Other Flippin family descendants involved with the business include Marcus' uncle James Flippin, his father Harold 'Jug' Flippin, his grandfather Joseph Paul Flippin, and his great grandfather Tilden Flippin.

James Flippin recalls memories of his grandfather, Tilden Flippin, farming on the White River, working for the railroad, the Army Corp of Engineers, and as a well driller. His brother, Harold Flippin is known as 'Jug' Flippin, due to the fact that school mates called him 'Little Brown Jug'. His father, Joseph Paul Flippin, worked as a steam fitter during the construction of the Bull Shoals and Norfolk dams, and as a well driller.

In the 1940's, when James and Harold Flippin were children, Flippin had a train depot, three grocery stores, two drug stores, a bank, post office, movie theater, hardware store, blacksmith shop and a jail house. The streets were not paved and there was a water well in the middle of the road in front of Sanders General Merchandise store.

Flippin Old Citizen's Bank

Buttermilk Biscuits   Edith Williams

2 cups all-purpose flour
1 1/2 tsp baking powder
1/2 tsp salt

1/3 cup shortening
3/4 cup buttermilk

In a bowl, combine flour, baking powder and salt. Cut in the shortening until crumbly. Stir in the buttermilk, just until moistened. Knead on a floured surface for 1 minute. Roll out into 1/2 inch thickness. Cut with a 2 1/2-inch biscuit cutter. Place on a greased baking sheet Bake at 450° F for 10–12 minutes or until golden brown.

Persimmon Quick Bread   Barbara Linde, Ph.D.

My neighbor in California gave me many persimmons. Sometimes I measured the persimmons out to 1 cup quantities and froze them in small containers. Then at special times, I could take out the container and make a persimmon bread loaf.

1 tsp baking soda
1 1/2 cups flour
1/2 cup brown sugar
1 tsp salt
1 tsp nutmeg (ground)
1/3 cup milk
1 cup nuts (chopped)

1 cup persimmon puree
1/2 cup granulated sugar
2 1/2 tsp baking powder
2 tsp cinnamon (ground)
1 egg
3 tbsp vegetable oil

Stir baking soda into persimmon puree and let stand for 5 minutes. In a bowl, combine flour, sugars, baking powder, salt, cinnamon and nutmeg. Set aside. In a large bowl, beat together egg, milk, oil and persimmon mixture. Add flour mixture and stir just until blended. Stir in nuts. Spoon mixture evenly into a greased 5x9-inch loaf pan. Bake in oven at 350° F until a wooden pick inserted in the center comes out clean, about 1 1/4 hours. Let cool at least 15 minutes; then turn out of pan onto a rack and let cool. Makes 1 loaf.

Pineapple Banana Nut Bread — Sandy Garrison

I created this recipe when I realized that I didn't have enough bananas to make the recipe correctly one day!

4 cups flour	2 1/2 cups sugar
1 tsp salt	1 tsp baking soda
1 cup butter flavor shortening	1 tsp vanilla extract
4 eggs	2 mashed bananas
1 (20 oz) can crushed pineapple (drained)	
1 cup pecans (chopped)	

Cream sugar and shortening. Sift dry ingredients. Beat in eggs and vanilla. Slowly mix dry ingredients with bananas and pineapple. Bake in 2 greased loaf pans at 300° F for about an hour.

A plentiful fall harvest in the Ozarks is persimmons. After frost these delicacies make scrumptious feasts. The persimmon has a prominent place in many Ozarkian kitchens. These tasty morsels will convince you that in the Ozarks, we know how to eat!

Refrigerator Rolls — Edith Williams

1 pkg yeast	1/4 cup sugar
1/4 cup warm water	1 tsp salt
3/4 cup milk (scalded)	3-3 1/2 cups flour
1/4 cup shortening	1 egg

Dissolve yeast in warm water. Mix shortening, sugar and salt in a bowl. Pour milk over this mixture. Mix in 1 cup of the flour and the egg. Add yeast and remaining flour. Mix well. Grease dough lightly and place in a bowl in the refrigerator for at least 3 hours. When ready to use, knead lightly, make into rolls and let rise in a warm place for 1 1/2 hours. Bake at 400° F until golden brown approximately 10-15 minutes.

English Muffin Loaf

Ethel Geving

Years ago, Linda Lobdell gave me this recipe. If you like English Muffins, you'll like this. Toast and slather with butter and or jam!!

4 1/2 - 5 cups flour, divided
2 tbsp yeast
1 tbsp sugar
2 tsp salt
1/4 tsp baking soda

2 cups milk
1/2 cup water (120° F)
corn meal

Mix 2 cups flour, yeast, sugar, salt and baking soda in a large bowl. Heat milk and water to 120° F. Add the warmed liquid to the flour mixture and stir well. Gradually add in 2 to 3 additional cups of flour until you form a stiff batter. Grease 2 glass or microwave safe 8 1/2x4 1/2-inch pans. Sprinkle greased pans with corn meal. Cut dough in half and form each into a loaf. Add dough to pans, cover and let rise in a cool, dry place for 45 minutes. Cook in your microwave oven on high heat for 6-6 1/2 minutes – no longer! Makes 2 loaves.

Bread Making Tips

Use a metal ice tray divider to cut biscuits in a hurry. Press into the dough and biscuits will separate at dividing lines when baked.

To make your own self-rising flour, mix 4 cups flour, 2 teaspoons salt, and 2 tablespoons baking powder. Store in a tightly covered container.

When in doubt, always sift flour before measuring.
When baking bread, you get a finer texture if you use milk. Water makes coarser bread.
For a quick, low-fat crunchy topping for muffins, sprinkle the tops with Grape-Nuts cereal before baking

Bunko Buns

Judy Martin

1 pkg party rolls (24)
1/4 stick butter (softened)
2 tbsp poppy seeds
2 tbsp mustard

1 small onion (minced)
4 oz. sliced ham
4 oz. sliced Swiss cheese
2 tbsp Worcestershire sauce

In a medium bowl, thoroughly mix butter, poppy seeds, mustard, Worcestershire sauce and onions. Spread butter mixture on the inside of both layers of sliced rolls. Place a layer of ham, then cheese on the bottom piece of bread. Cover with top piece of bread. Place on a cookie sheet and cover with foil. Bake a 350° F for 15-20 minutes, until cheese melts. Serve warm! Makes 24 sandwiches.

> To make quick and easy bread crumbs, toast the heels of your bread and chop in a blender or food processor!

Brown Bread

Sibyl Dardin

This recipe came from a cookbook which was compiled by The Eastern Star in the early 1960's. The recipe is from Mildred Shaw, a longtime resident of Flippin.

2 cups graham flour
4 tsp baking soda
2 cups raisins
3 cups sour milk

2 cups white flour (all-purpose)
   pinch of salt
1 cup molasses

Sift together the dry ingredients. Add molasses and sour milk. Mix thoroughly. Turn into a greased bread pan and let stand covered for 1 hour. Bake at 325° F for 1 hour. Turn bread and pan upside down after removing from the oven and leave until cool – this makes the bread moist! Makes 2 loaves.

> When baking bread, a small dish of water in the oven will help keep the crust from getting too hard or brown.

Holiday Hot Rolls
Deloris Sanders

After learning how to make these rolls when I was a teenager working in a café in Yellville, Arkansas, I taught my mother, Ivon Johnson, to prepare the rolls. She then made them for my boyfriend, A.J. Sanders' first dinner in our home. After marrying A.J. of Flippin in 1941, these rolls became part of the Bonnie and Lester Sanders' family holiday dinners. Our granddaughter in South Carolina, Stacy Sanders Hall, continues the tradition by making these rolls to celebrate family gatherings.

1 pkg dry yeast	1 tsp salt
2 cups lukewarm water	7 cups flour, divided
2 eggs (unbeaten)	melted butter
1/2 cup sugar	2/3 cup shortening

Add yeast to lukewarm water, mixing until yeast dissolves. Add eggs, sugar, shortening and salt. Stir well. Sift in 4 cups of flour and stir well. Add the remaining 3 cups of flour, 1 cup at a time and stir well. Cover and place in refrigerator overnight. When ready to use, remove desired amount of dough and allow to rise for 4 hours. Knead to get air out. Roll dough out 1/4-1/2 inch thick. Cut out biscuit shapes with a small glass or biscuit cutter. Dip both sides of each roll in melted butter, fold over and place in a greased pan. Let rise until doubled in size (about 40 minutes) in a warm place. Bake at 400° F for 15-20 minutes. Enjoy! Makes 2-3 dozen.

Basic Sourdough Starter
Angela Ilacqua

1 cup flour	1 cup water
1 tbsp sugar	4 tbsp buttermilk

Mix ingredients in a glass container; cover with a towel and let stand in a warm place for a few days until it has begun to ferment. As it begins to sour it will have a consistency of butter. Cover and store in refrigerator. Each time you take out a helping of the starter, you need to replenish it with the same amount of flour and water.

Southern Biscuits

Lee Powell

My grandfather loved his biscuits. His mother made these for him as he grew up, then my grandmother kept up the tradition.

2 cups sifted all-purpose flour **3 tsp baking powder**
1/2 tsp salt **1/3 cup shortening**
3/4 cup buttermilk

Sift dry ingredients into a bowl, cut in the shortening till like coarse meal. Make a well; add milk all at once. Stir quickly with fork just until dough follows fork around the bowl. Turn onto lightly floured surface. Dough should be soft, knead gently 10-12 strokes. Roll dough to ½ inch thick. Dip biscuit cutter in flour; cut straight down. (At this point you can bag the biscuits and flash freeze for later use). Bake at 450° F for 10-12 minutes on ungreased baking sheet. Makes about 10 biscuits.

> If your biscuits are dry, it could be from too much handling, or the oven temperature may not have been hot enough.

Pineapple Biscuits

Brenda Rowden

My mom made these when I was a kid and they are so good to have anytime and so cheap to make!

1 can biscuits **1/2 cup brown sugar**
2 tbsp butter
1 large can crushed pineapple (drained)

Put pineapple, brown sugar and butter in a sauce pan. Heat to boiling. Spray a 9x9-inch square pan well with nonstick spray. Pour pineapple mixture in baking pan and place biscuits on top of pineapple. Bake until biscuits are done (10–15 minutes). Makes 10 biscuits.

Mexican Cornbread
Edith Williams

1/2 cup margarine
2 eggs
1 (4 oz) can minced green chilies
1/2 cup cheddar cheese (grated)
1/4 tsp salt
1 cup corn meal
1/2 cup milk

1/4 cup sugar
1 (no. 303) can cream corn

1 cup flour
2 tsp baking powder

Cream margarine and sugar. Add remaining ingredients. Pour mixture into a greased large black cast iron skillet. Bake at 350° F for 45–50 minutes.

Sharon's Zucchini Bread
Ethel Geving

My sister, Sharon gave me this recipe years ago and being able to toss all the ingredients into the blender was great. Sharon put it all in the blender except the nuts and raisins. Of course, if you add nuts and raisins, stir them in after blending!

2 cups zucchini
3 eggs
3 cups flour
1 1/2 cups sugar
1 tsp baking soda

1 tsp salt
1 tbsp cinnamon
3/4 cup oil
1 cup walnuts, (optional)
1 cup raisins, (optional)

Place unpeeled zucchini and eggs in a blender. Mix the remaining ingredients in a large bowl. Add to egg mixture. Blend well. Stir in nuts and raisins (optional). Pour mixture into 2 bread pans and bake at 350° F for 1 hour or more. Makes 2 loaves.

> To take full advantage of the abundance of Zucchini when it is in season, try freezing it. Choose young, tender zucchini. Wash and cut in ½-inch slices. Blanch in boiling water for 3 minutes. Cool promptly in ice-cold water before draining and packaging in freezer bags or containers, leaving 1/2-inch headspace. Seal and freeze.

"Baseball Bat" Zucchini Bread   Linda Armstrong

As a child, my father always grew zucchini plants in his garden, so I planted several plants in my first vegetable garden. I was pleased to see tiny, green zucchini squashes growing on my vines. However, a day or so later I was shocked to discover my tiny zucchini squashes had grown very large, the size of baseball bats!

3 eggs   1/4 cup oil
2/3 cup applesauce   1/3 cup white sugar
3/4 cup brown sugar   1 tbsp vanilla extract
1 tsp baking soda   1 tbsp cinnamon
1/2 tsp baking powder   1/2 tsp nutmeg
2 1/2 cups grated zucchini   2 cups white flour (all purpose)
1 cup wheat flour

Chocolate Chip Zucchini Bread
Add these extra ingredients to the original recipe:
3/4 tsp baking powder   12 oz (2 cups) chocolate chips
3 tbsp baking cocoa

Peel and remove the seeds (only from a larger squash), then grate the squash. Drain away any liquid. In a large electric mixer bowl add together eggs, oil and applesauce. Mix on medium speed until blended. Add white sugar, brown sugar, baking soda, cinnamon, baking powder and nutmeg. Mix well. Add grated zucchini. Mix well. While mixer is running on the lower speed, gradually add flours. Mix well on medium speed. Prepare 2, 9x5x3-inch loaf pans by greasing and lining the bottom of the pans with wax paper. Fill loaf pans 2/3 full. Bake at 325° F for 1 hour. Bake just until a toothpick inserted does not have liquid batter on it. Be careful not to over bake! Cool on cooling rack for 5-10 minutes. Loosen bread from side of loaf pan with a knife. Remove the bread from pan, remove wax paper and place on cooling rack. Loosely cover breads with plastic wrap and allow to cool completely. When cool, wrap breads in plastic wrap or put in a closed plastic bag. Zucchini bread is best served after being wrapped in plastic for 24 hours, allowing the bread to become more moist. Top zucchini bread slices with butter. Makes 2 loaves.

Pawpaw Bread
Connie Ply

Pawpaws are available at the farmer's markets normally in the fall. Fill a brown paper lunch sack with pawpaws. If they are not all ripe at the same time (they usually aren't), put the ripe ones in a tightly sealed plastic bag in the fridge and they will wait for the others. A pawpaw is ripe when it is easily dented with your finger.

2/3 cup canola oil
4 large eggs (or 6 small)
3 1/2 cups whole wheat pastry flour
2 tsp baking powder
1 tsp soda
1/2 tsp salt
1 paper lunch sack full of pawpaws
1/3 cup honey (use 2/3 for a cake-like sweetness)

Cut the pawpaws open with a paring knife, dig the seeds out, and scrape the fruit into a bowl. Mash the pawpaws with a potato masher or a fork. Add oil and eggs to the pawpaw and mix. Mix the flour, soda, baking powder and salt together. Add to pawpaw mixture and mix just until it's all combined. Pour into two oiled loaf pans. Bake at 350° F for 45-50 minutes, until a toothpick comes out clean. Be careful not to over bake; it gets dry easily.

Breads made from scratch or from a mix must have an internal temperature of about 80 degrees for the yeast to work properly. Cold dough will not expand properly. Make sure the bread rises in a warm, draft free environment.

BREAKFAST

Flippin School...In The Beginning

The first Flippin school was a large one-room building that doubled as a church. Soon after the railroad was completed in 1904, the school house was moved near the "new town" of Flippin. As the attendance grew more rooms were added as well as a drilled well with a hand pump. Four "little houses" (outhouses) lined nearby Crane Creek.

The school had a large yard where baseball, pole vaulting, broad jumps and basketball were played while the younger children made playhouses and played games at recess. During the lunch hour teachers and students went outside in the shade to eat. Generally, several children in a family had all their lunches packed together in one eight-pound lard bucket. Lunch was usually sweetnins' (molasses and butter stirred together), a cold biscuit and maybe a sweet potato, a fresh tomato, fried chicken, corn on the cob, cookies or a fried pie.

The school term was usually divided with the three months of July, August, and September as a vacation for the children to help their families pick cotton. Subjects consisted of the three R's (readin', 'ritin' and 'rithmetic) plus physiology, geography, spelling, precision marching, track meets and literary meets. The pupils were expected to furnish their own books, paper and pencils.

A new school building was constructed in 1928. It had no inside plumbing and was heated with huge wood stoves. The first graduating class from the new Flippin school was in the spring of 1929.

During a cold, windy, rainy night, on February 13, 1951, the school building burned to the ground when a wood stove overheated. The present main Flippin school building was built on the same foundation.

Flippin School, built in 1928. Burned February 13, 1951

The Johnston and
The McCracken Families

A Part of the Fabric of Flippin

The mayor of Flippin Arkansas, Mary Jane Erwin, comes from a long line of public servants on both sides of her family tree. Her grandfather represents the McCracken family and her father comes from the Johnston family. Both of these families are among the original families who were here when Flippin came into being in the early 1800's.

The Mayor's father, R.W. (Rudy) Johnston, moved to Flippin in 1948 when he married Mary Jane's mother, Wanda Lee McCracken

Mayor Mary Jane Erwin

Johnston who worked as an assistant Postmaster for many years in Flippin. Her father served on the City Council for more than 30 years. Her grandfather, Gus McCracken served the community as Sheriff, Judge and as State Representative of Marion County throughout a lifetime of public service.

In addition to coming from two of the oldest families in Flippin, Mary Jane Erwin was born and raised right here in Flippin. She has served as the Clerk and Mayor of Flippin since 1992.

The Johnstons and the McCracken families, including

26

Mary Jane, have participated in many volunteer organizations over the years. They have worked to help bring new business to town while maintaining that small town feel.

When asked how Mary Jane feels about her hometown, she answered, "Flippin is home. It is beautiful country, has the most wonderful people in the world and is a community that cares for each other. Flippin has grown by leaps and bounds with industry and commercial business, but it still retains the small town atmosphere of caring and sharing."

The Johnston and the McCracken families represent all that is good about small town living. They participate in the process and aren't afraid to roll up their sleeves to pitch in and get the job done. They care about their community enough to make a career out of public service. "Flippin is dear to my heart and the greatest place in the world to live." said Mary Jane Erwin, Mayor of Flippin Arkansas.

Johnston Pineapple Salad   Mary Jane Erwin

This recipe came from my father's family, Rudy Johnston. It is very different, but very delicious.

1/2 lb American cheese (grated)   **3 bananas (sliced)**
1 small can pineapple tidbits   **2 pickles (grated)**
3 boiled eggs (chopped)   **mayonnaise to taste**

Mix together grated cheese, drained pineapple tidbits, chopped eggs, bananas sliced and grated pickles. Add mayonnaise to taste for texture.

Breakfast Casserole

Patsy R. Johnson

1 lb sliced bacon
2 cups ham (chopped)
1 large onion (chopped)
10 slices of white bread
1 tbsp Worcestershire sauce
2 cups potatoes (cooked, cut into cubes)
12 oz cheddar cheese (shredded)
1 pinch of salt & pepper

8 eggs
3 cups milk
1 tsp dry mustard

Prepare the bread by removing the crusts and cut into small cubes. Cook bacon until crisp, drain and crumble when cool. Set aside. Add ham and onion to skillet. Cook, stirring occasionally, until onion is tender. Drain this mixture. In a greased 9x13x2-inch baking dish, make layers using half the bread cubes, ham, bacon and onion mixture, ending with cheese. In a bowl, beat eggs. To this mixture, add milk, Worcestershire sauce, mustard, salt and pepper. Stir well. Pour this mixture over the top of the casserole. Cover dish and chill overnight. Remove from refrigerator 30 minutes before baking. Bake uncovered at 350° F 35 – 45 minutes. Makes 12 servings.

100 Percent Bran Flakes Muffins

Bennie Sue Williams-Hunter

1 cup shortening
4 eggs (beaten)
5 cups flour (all-purpose)
1 tsp salt
2 cups boiling water

3 cups sugar
1 qt buttermilk
5 tsp baking soda
6 cups All Bran flakes

Pour boiling water over flakes. Let cool. Cream shortening and sugar. Add beaten eggs and buttermilk, stirring constantly. Stir in the cooled All Bran flakes. Sift flour into buttermilk mixture. Fold in all of the flour until well mixed. Store in air-tight covered container in the refrigerator until you are ready to bake. Batter will keep for up to 6 weeks or longer. Bake muffins as desired in a preheated 400° F oven for 20 to 30 minutes.

Cowboy Scramble
Lynne Moore

We know there are a million variations of this. But this recipe is very good with eggs, new potatoes and cheddar cheese. This makes a great breakfast but don't overlook it for lunch or even dinner. And it's quick and easy, ready to go in maybe 15 minutes. This dish is very good and is a keeper!

1 tbsp butter	1/2 large onion (diced)

1/2 green or red bell pepper (chopped)
8 large eggs

1/2 cup cheddar cheese (grated)	1/2 tsp dry basil leaves
1/4 cup cilantro leaves (chopped)	1/2 tsp salt

1/4 tsp pepper
1/2 cup cheddar cheese (grated)
3-4 cups new red potatoes (unpeeled, diced to 3/8 inch)
1/3 pound fried and crumbled bacon

In the butter, sauté over medium heat the onion, potatoes and pepper until the potatoes are almost tender. While the vegetables are cooking, mix the eggs, 1/4 cup cheddar cheese, basil, cilantro, salt and pepper in a bowl. Once the potatoes are nearly cooked, pour the egg mixture over the vegetables. Turn the heat down and continue cooking, while stirring often, until the eggs are done. This dish can be served from the skillet or from a platter. Immediately after cooking, sprinkle the remaining 1/4 cup cheddar cheese over the scramble and let it melt.

'Oh Boy' Waffles
Rita Ross

2 1/4 cups flour(all-purpose)	4 tsp baking powder
3/4 tsp salt	1 1/2 tbsp sugar
2 eggs (beaten)	2 1/4 cups milk
1/4 cup salad oil	1 tsp vanilla extract

Whisk together dry ingredients. Combine eggs, milk, oil and vanilla. Add to dry ingredients, beating only till moistened (batter will be thin). Bake in preheated waffle baker. Makes 10-12 waffles.

Pecan French Toast

Ann Glueck

I was given this recipe from a friend and have enjoyed using it when there is a group/family together for breakfast. Since it is baked, there is less mess to cook it and it frees me up to other things - like enjoy my guests and family.

4 eggs
1/3 cup milk
1/4 tsp nutmeg
1/2 cup pecan pieces
1/2 cup butter or margarine (melted)
1/2 (8 oz) loaf Italian bread (cut into 1 inch slices)
2 tbsp grated orange peel, to taste (approximately)
cinnamon (optional)

2/3 cup orange juice
1/4 cup sugar
1/4 tsp vanilla extract

Using a wire whisk, beat together eggs, orange juice, milk, sugar, nutmeg and vanilla extract. Place bread with edges touching in a single layer in a large flat dish. Pour liquid mixture over the bread, cover and refrigerate overnight, turning 1 time. When ready to cook, pour melted butter in a jelly roll pan, spreading evenly. Arrange soaked bread slices in a single layer on the pan. Sprinkle evenly with orange peel and pecans. (I also sprinkle with cinnamon). Bake at 400° F until golden, 20–25 minutes. Check slices during final 10 minutes of baking to avoid burning. Serve with maple syrup and butter or fresh fruit. Makes 4 servings.

Breakfast Grits

Ina Johnson

1 1/2 cups milk
2 cups boiling water
pepper to taste
1 cup stone-ground or other good quality grits

4 tablespoons butter
1 teaspoon salt

In the top of a double boiler, stir the milk into the grits, then add the water and seasonings. Stir well, cover tightly and place over the bottom, filled with an inch or two of boiling water. Cook over low heat anywhere from 45 minutes to an 1 1/2 hours, or more, depending on the coarseness of the grind. When the grits are soft, add butter and serve. Serves 4.

Raspberry Cheesecake Muffins   Lynne Moore

3 oz cream cheese	3 eggs, divided
1 cup sugar	1 cup milk
1 1/2 tsp vanilla extract, divided	6 tbsp butter
2 1/2 tsp baking powder	2 cup flour
1/2 tsp salt	1 cup raspberries

Grease muffin tins or line with paper cups. In a small bowl, beat together until smooth, the cream cheese with 1 egg, 1/4 cup sugar and 1/2 tsp vanilla and set aside. In a saucepan, combine the milk, butter and 1 tsp vanilla. Stir over medium heat until the butter melts. Cool until warm to the touch, then beat in the remaining 2 eggs. In a large bowl, combine the flour, baking powder, salt and remaining sugar. Add the milk mixture and stir just to blend. Fold in the raspberries. Divide the batter equally among the muffin cups. Spoon about 2 teaspoons of the cream cheese mixture on top of each muffin. Pull knife through each top to swirl slightly. Bake at 400° F for 20 minutes or until top springs back when lightly touched.

Apple, Sage & Fennel Breakfast Sausage   Ina Johnson

This is a wonderful mix of flavors!

2 tbsp dried onions	1/4 + 1/8 tsp ground sage
1 1/2 + 1/8 tsp ground fennel	
1/16 tsp salt	
1/8 tsp onion powder	1/16 black pepper
1 lb ground pork	1 medium granny smith apple

Mix spices and seasonings into ground pork. Peel, core and finely dice apple (use a handy chopper or food processor). Microwave chopped apple in covered dish for approximately 2 minutes at 1/2 power until softened, but not fully cooked. Cool apples. Mix apples into pork. Form into patties with hamburger press, or by hand. Fry, broil or grill on tabletop grill (i.e. Farberware). Cook just until done.

Broccoli and Ham Quiche

Sarah Bond

This is good for Sunday brunch. Smells so good while it's baking!

1/2 pkg refrigerated pie crust
1/2 cup instant potato flakes
1 can cream of celery soup
1 garlic clove (pressed)
1 tsp dill seasoning (optional)
3/4 cup Swiss or cheddar cheese
8 cherry tomatoes (optional)
1 (9 oz) pkg broccoli florets (thawed, drained and chopped)

3 eggs
3/4 cup deli ham (diced)
1 tsp Dijon mustard

Unfold crust and roll out. Then place crust in a deep dish pie pan. In a small bowl, whisk eggs, set aside. In another bowl mix broccoli and ham, soup, mustard, garlic, potato flakes and dill (optional) then microwave for 4 minutes or until hot. Add eggs, stir well then add cheese. Pour this mixture into pie shell. Cut tomatoes in half and arrange on top of filling in a circular pattern. Bake at 400° F for 35-40 minutes or until golden brown.

Light and Wonderful Pancakes

Angela Ilacqua

3/4 cup self-rising flour
3/4 cup whole wheat flour
1 tsp baking soda
1 1/2 cups 1% milk
1 tsp vanilla extract
1 tbsp oil
blueberries (optional - fresh or if frozen, thawed)

1/2 cup white flour
2 tsp baking powder
1 egg
3/4 cup light sour cream
2 tsp sugar

Whisk together flours, baking soda and baking powder. In a separate bowl combine egg, milk, sour cream, vanilla, sugar and oil. Add to dry ingredients and stir gently until just combined. Pour batter onto preheated medium hot griddle. Drop blueberries onto pancakes. Turn when lightly browned on underside. Makes 6-plate-sized pancakes.

New Orleans Beignets
Mike Osmundson

Café Du Monde is the Original French Market Coffee Stand and since 1862 has been serving Biegnets and Café Au Lait across from Jackson Square in the New Orleans French Quarter. Beignets are puffy square French donuts, served hot in orders of 3 to a plate, generously covered with powdered sugar. Café Du Monde was spared from destruction by hurricane Katrina in 2005 and today still serves their famous Beignets.

1 package dry yeast	4 tbsp warm water
3 1/2 cups plus 2 tbsp flour	1 tsp salt
1/4 cup sugar	1 1/4 cup milk
3 eggs, beaten	1/4 cup melted butter
vegetable oil	powdered sugar

In a measuring cup combine the yeast and warm water. Stir to blend well then set aside. In a large mixing bowl, combine flour, salt and sugar. Using a wire whisk, stir until all ingredients are well blended. Add blossomed yeast, milk, eggs and butter. Mix with a wooden spoon until dough has formed. Cover dough with a dish towel and set in a warm place. Allow dough to rise for 1 hour. Pour vegetable oil into a home style deep fryer, such as a Fry Daddy and heat to 350° F. Dust a work surface with additional flour and turn the dough onto the floured surface. Knead dough once or twice and roll out to approximately 1/3 to 1/2-inch thickness. Cut dough into 3-inch squares and return to a lightly floured pan. Allow the doughnut to rest, covered for approximately 10 minutes. Deep fry the beignets, 2-3 at a time, for approximately 2 minutes on each side or until golden brown and puffed. Remove beignets from oil, drain and dust generously with powdered sugar. Serves: 10-12, 3 beignets per serving.

Egg Tips
A fresh egg will sink in water, a stale one will float.
For light, fluffy scrambled eggs, add a little water while beating the eggs.
Add vinegar to the water when boiling eggs. The vinegar helps seal the egg.

Razorback Breakfast Casserole
Karen Shelby

Serve with fresh fruit, hash browns and your favorite breakfast drinks.

1 cup milk	1 cup cream
6 eggs (beaten)	1 tsp black pepper
1 tbsp yellow mustard	1 tsp salt
2 cups cheddar cheese (grated)	1 cup mushrooms (sliced)

6-8 slices of bread (crusts removed and cubed)
1 lb pork sausage (cooked, crumbled and drained)
1/2 lb bacon (cooked, crumbled and drained)

Spray a 9x13-inch pan with non-stick cooking spray. Spread bread cubes evenly over the bottom of the pan. Sprinkle the crumbled sausage and bacon over the bread, then sprinkle the grated cheese and mushrooms over the meat. In a medium bowl, combine the beaten eggs, mustard, salt & pepper, cream and milk, mix well. Pour the egg mixture over the other ingredients in the 9x13-inch pan. Cover and refrigerate overnight. To bake, preheat oven to 350° F. Uncover casserole and place in preheated oven. Bake uncovered 35-40 minutes or until eggs are firm. Let stand 5 minutes before slicing.

Cinnamon Rolls
Sandra Treat Roberts

These are great for breakfast!

1 tsp cinnamon	1/2 stick margarine
1/2 cup nuts	3/4 cup brown sugar (packed)

18 frozen dinner rolls (I use Bridgford)
1 box butterscotch pudding (not instant)

Spray bundt pan with Pam, or other non-stick spray. Place frozen dinner rolls around in pan. Sprinkle dry butterscotch pudding, brown sugar and cinnamon on rolls. Sprinkle nuts on ingredients. Melt margarine and pour it over the above. Cover with a tea towel and let it set overnight (6–8 hours). Bake at 375° F for about 30 minutes.

Sandra Treat Roberts is the granddaughter of Ida And William Treat.

SOUPS & SALADS

The "Barn"

The Barn was just not any barn, but one located on Highway 178 in Flippin, Arkansas, across the street from the Flippin High School. With high visibility, it was used by senior classes from Flippin, Yellville-Summit, Cotter and Mountain Home schools to make their 'mark', a school spirited statement for everyone to see. Passerbys grew accustomed to reading the rite-of-passage graffiti, such as "Seniors Rule", "Class of 2004", "Seniors Rock" or the graffiti writers' mascot, whether the Flippin Bobcats, or nearby schools' Panthers, or Bombers.

Painting the barn was considered a battle by students to be the "top coat", covering the endeavor of the previous artist's work. The barn received a fresh look in 2003 in preparation for Flippin's Ranger Rally Days, when the entire structure was painted and the Ranger logo painted on the roof. Many thought the graffiti would end, but students "considered that a challenge" and the graffiti continued.

The original structure of the barn was constructed in 1886, and had been added onto through the years. The barn was burned in October, 2005 due to safety concerns by the owner.

Violet Hensley: Arkansas Living Legend

The Whittling Fiddler of Yellville, Arkansas

Since the 1960's Arkansas fiddler and fiddle maker Violet Hensley has earned national renown. Given the nickname, the "Whittling Fiddler", Violet Hensley has appeared on national television on shows from the Beverly Hillbillies, Art Linkletter, Charles Kuralt's On the Road, Captain Kangaroo, To Tell the Truth, to Tokyo, Japan's 60 Minutes. She has also tirelessly performed and demonstrated her craft at festivals, schools, colleges, nursing homes, made appearances throughout the West and Midwest and promoted Silver Dollar City in Branson, Missouri. Many periodicals from the local to the national level have run features on her, from National Geographic and Modern Maturity to Country America.

Born in 1916 on the family homestead near Mount Ida, Arkansas, Violet learned to carve fiddles while still a teenager from her father, George Washington Brumley (usually know as 'Wash') who made his first fiddle in 1888 when he was fourteen. Following in her father's footsteps, she learned to play when she was twelve, learning her oldest tunes from him and her neighbors. Violet made her first fiddle when she was fifteen. "I learned by helping my daddy. He never showed me how to make one when I decided I could make one. I just learned by helping him."

Before radio and television every Ozark community had a fiddler who attended all the parties, dances, barn warmings, pie suppers and social gatherings. Unable to read a note of music these fiddlers, accompanied by a guitar, banjo or mandolin, claimed they could play all night and never repeat the same song. Frequently, they did.

Violet still continues to play the fourth fiddle she made. In order to make a fiddle, Hensley has been known to use a crosscut saw to fell trees and dry the wood by the fireplace. She completes the process by using hand planes, keyhole saws, homemade curved knives and various hand tools. She has developed her craft to a fine art. Each fiddle is lovingly crafted to perfection. Violet has a total of 73 fiddles to her credit. Owners of Hensley fiddles include Jimmy Driftwood, Lonnie Robertson and Chubby Wise. One of her hand made fiddles was played at the Grand Ol' Opry by Senator Robert Byrd.

Known as the "Stradivarius of the Ozarks," her fiddle making caught the attention of the folks at the new Silver Dollar City in Branson, Missouri in the 1960's and now is home to Hensley during its annual National Crafts Festival each fall. Since 1967 she has demonstrated her craft there during 39 consecutive festivals.

In 2004, Mrs. Hensley received the Living Treasure Award from the Arkansas Arts Council. To commemorate the honor, she received a plaque, which honored her for a lifetime of achievement. The award is presented to an Arkansan who is outstanding in the creation of a traditional craft and has elevated their work to the status of art and actively preserves and advances the art form. Nearly 200 members of her community gathered to help her celebrate as she and her family gave a performance that included tunes she has known since the 1920's— "Little Brown Jug" and "Eighth of January."

Violet quit playing and making fiddles for twenty-seven years between making her fourth and fifth fiddle to raise her nine children. "I hardly even picked my fiddle up during that time. In fact, it wasn't even strung up." Violet laughed as she showed her first fiddle, "What's left of it. Two of my boys busted it all to pieces."

Violet Hensley

One of Violet's favorite recipes from the 1940's, Potatoes and Carrots, is located on page 62.

Do-Ahead Cabbage Salad

Sherry Berthot

This recipe was my grandmother Babcock's. Always a favorite at family gatherings.

1 medium cabbage head
1 onion
1/2 bunch celery
1 carrot
1 green pepper
1 tsp salt

1/2-1 cup sugar
1/4 cup vegetable oil
1/2 cup white vinegar
1 tsp celery seed
1 tsp mustard seed

Chop all vegetables fine. Add vinegar and other ingredients. Put in tightly covered jar. Keep in refrigerator. Will keep crisp and good about 1 week.

Taffy Apple Salad

Theresa M. Baldridge

This is always a favorite at family get-togethers. Tastes just like a taffy apple!

1 lg can chunky pineapple
2 cups mini-marshmallows
1/2 cup sugar
1 1/2 cups Spanish nuts
3 1/2 cups apples (unpeeled, diced)

1 1/2 tsp vinegar
1 lg container Cool Whip
1 tbsp flour
1 egg (well beaten)

Drain pineapple and save juice. Combine drained pineapple with marshmallows. Refrigerate overnight. In a saucepan over medium heat, mix together pineapple juice, sugar, flour, well beaten egg and vinegar until sugar is melted and sauce thickens. Refrigerate overnight. Mix sauce with Cool Whip and add remaining ingredients. Mix well. Refrigerate for 8 hours.

> Perk up soggy lettuce by soaking it in a mixture of lemon juice and cold water.

Cauliflower Salad
Irma Zurn

This recipe was from my mom's sorority sister. It's been getting raves for 40 years.

1 head lettuce
1 box frozen peas
1/2 cup chopped onion
1/2 cup parmesan cheese
1 pkg Good Seasons (dry mix) garlic-cheese dressing

1 pint mayonnaise
1 head of cauliflower
1 lb bacon (fried crisp)

Layer lettuce, peas, cauliflower, onion, bacon in order in a large Tupperware bowl with a lid. Spread mayo over like frosting a cake. Sprinkle on Good Season's dressing and Parmesan cheese. Seal and refrigerate overnight. Toss 1 hour before serving.

Cranberry Fluff
Myrt Flippin

2 cups raw cranberries (ground)
1/4 tsp salt
1/2 cup seedless green grapes
2 cups apples (diced, unpared)
3 cups tiny (mini) marshmallows
1/2 cup broken english walnuts
1 cup heavy cream (whipped or use Cool Whip instead)

Combine cranberries, sugar and marshmallows, stirring well. Cover and chill overnight. Add apples, grapes, walnuts and salt, mixing until well combined. Fold in whipped cream. Chill. Turn into serving bowl or individual lettuce cups. Garnish with green grapes. Makes 8-10 servings.

Party Pink Salad
Elaine Slavings

1 can cherry pie filling
1/2 bag small marshmallows
1 can sweetened condensed milk
1 (15oz) can crushed pineapple
1 cup pecans
1 medium container cool whip

Drain pineapple. Mix all ingredients together. Refrigerate until ready to serve.

Pistachio Ambrosia

Heidi Bloxam

This is a wonderful party salad!

2 tsp orange extract
2/3 cup flaked coconut
2 (17 oz) cans of fruit cocktail
2 (20 oz) cans of pineapple chunks
2 (3.5 oz) pkg instant pistachio pudding mix
1 (16 oz) container of sour cream (2 cups)
1 (12 oz) container of Cool Whip (regular, light or free)
1 cup walnuts or pecans (chopped)

Drain fruit cocktail and pineapple together, reserving juices. Set fruit aside. Measure 1 1/2 cups of juice and pour into a 4-quart bowl. Add pudding mix and mix until smooth. Stir in sour cream. Add Cool Whip and mix until smooth. Fold in fruit, nuts and coconut. Transfer salad to decorative serving bowl. Cover and chill for several hours. Top with chopped walnuts or pecans just before serving. Serves 16-20.

Italian Pasta Salad

Stacie Hopper

1 bag tri-colored Rotini noodles
1 can diced tomatoes
1 can sliced black olives (drained)
1 bottle of Italian dressing
1 pkg sliced pepperoni
1 bag Swiss cheese (shredded)
bacon bits (optional topping)

Boil noodles for about 10 minutes, drain and put into a larger bowl. Mix in all ingredients. Add bacon bits to the top if desired. Chill for a couple of hours and serve.

Your fruit salads will look perfect when you use an egg slicer to make perfect slices of strawberries, kiwis, or bananas.

Secret Strawberry Salad Pearl Norcross

This is a quick – no cook recipe and you can make it ahead. It is an unusual blend of pleasing flavors and sure to please the healthy-food diner. The recipe dates back to the 1800's popular as a summer salad. Now-a-days fresh berries are available in grocery stores year-round so you can enjoy the festive bright red strawberries and delicate green celery salad during the winter holidays as well.

1/2 cup fresh strawberries (per person)
1/4 cup celery (per person)

Dressing:

6 tbsp olive oil	**1 tbsp salt**
2 tbsp lemon juice	**1/4 cup honey**
1/3 teaspoon paprika (secret ingredient)	

Cut strawberries in half long way, use 1/2 the amount of strawberries to cut celery, sliced thin or in short strips. Keep in separate bowls and set aside to chill. In mixing bowl, pour olive oil, salt, lemon juice, honey and the paprika. Beat 2 minutes or until frothy. Drain the strawberries and add celery to the bowl. Drench with honey dressing and mix.

Chicken Salad Gail Flippin

Canned chicken makes prep time even faster and tastes great! Sweet or tart apples can be used, depending on your taste.

2 cups chicken (cooked, chopped)	**2 tbsp plain yogurt**
3/4 cup apples (unpeeled, chopped)	**1 tsp lemon juice**
1/4 cup celery (chopped)	**1/8 tsp salt**
1/2 cup walnuts (chopped)	
1/2 cup Miracle Whip light mayonnaise	

Mix all ingredients. Chill. Serve between bread slices as a sandwich or in a dish on top of a lettuce leaf. Store in tightly covered container in refrigerator up to 2 days. Makes 6-8 servings.

Waldorf Fruit Salad
Dorothy Schill

This salad is an expanded version of the original Waldorf salad recipe. The Waldorf-Astoria Hotel in New York created this food classic in 1896. Originally, the salad was made with apples, celery and mayonnaise and around 1928 walnuts were added. The Waldorf Salad remains a favorite and is still featured on the hotel menu.

1/8 cup raisins
1 stalk celery (diced)
1/8 cup flaked coconut (optional)
1 banana (peeled, halved and sliced)
1 pear (unpeeled, cored and diced)
1 orange (peeled, sectioned and sliced)
1 cup green or red seedless grapes
1/4 cup walnuts or sunflower seeds (chopped)
1 golden delicious apple (unpeeled, cored and diced)
1-1 1/2 cups Miracle Whip mayonnaise
(this brand tastes the best; use regular, light or fat free)
white sugar or 'Splenda' to taste

Mix together fruit, celery, nuts and coconut in a large bowl. Add mayonnaise and mix together. Add enough mayonnaise to coat all of fruit mixture with dressing. If salad needs sweetening, sprinkle on a small amount of white sugar or 'Splenda' and mix in. Adjust to taste. Chill and serve. Serves 4-6.

Frozen Salad
Jane Herbst

1 (1 lb) can jellied cranberries
1 pkg dream whip (prepared)
1 can crushed pineapple (drained)

1/4 cup powdered sugar
1 cup sour cream

Combine above and freeze in muffin paper cups. Let stand at room temperature for 5 minutes before serving.

Zesty Pasta Salad
Elena Wilson

Desperate to find a unique dish for a pot luck occasion with new friends, I turned to my mother's recipe book and found "Zesty Pasta Salad." It sounded so good - and it was! This tasty recipe is now my favorite pot luck dish. Enjoy!

1/2 cup Miracle Whip mayonnaise
1 cup cherry tomatoes (halved)
1/4 cup parmesan cheese   1 cup green pepper chunks
2 tbsp milk   1/4 cup onions (chopped)
1/2 cup ham (cubed)   1/2 tsp salt
1 cup corkscrew pasta (cooked)   lettuce

Combine Miracle Whip, cheese and milk. Mix well. Add all the rest of the ingredients, except the lettuce - mix well. Chill. Add lettuce when ready to serve.

Red Cabbage and Apples
Carol Wulf

This dish I first had in a German restaurant, served with either Polish sausage or bratwurst. It is great with hot dogs, Kielbasa or pork chops. It is even good cold as a side dish!

1 small head of red cabbage   1 tbsp caraway seeds (optional)
3 medium apples   1 cup crisp bacon (optional)
1/2 cup sugar   1/2 cup vinegar
3/4 tsp ground cloves
Polish Sausage, Kielbasa, Bratwurst, (optional)

Core and thinly slice the cabbage. Peel and grate the apples and combine with the cabbage, sugar, vinegar, cloves and caraway seeds (optional). Simmer in a covered sauce pan for 1-2 hours or cook in a crock pot on medium or high heat for 5 hours – stirring occasionally. If desired, add hot dogs or sausages (Polish Kielbasa, Bratwurst) or sprinkle with bacon before serving.

Tomato, Cucumber & Apple Salad

Karen Shelby

3 tbsp olive oil
1/4 cup red wine vinegar
salt and pepper to taste
3 large ripe tomatoes (rough chopped)
1 cucumber (peeled and cut in 1/2 inch cubes)
1 sweet apple (peeled, cored and diced)
Large lettuce leaves for serving

Combine the tomatoes, cucumber and apples in a large bowl. Toss all together and season with salt and pepper. Drizzle with red wine vinegar and olive oil, toss again to combine and adjust seasoning. Serve on lettuce leaves. *This salad recipe is a perfect compliment to Karen's Moroccan Venison recipe on page 70.*

Aunt Minnie Salad

Shelly Daniel Xiques

Aunt Minnie Mohler was the sister of my grandmother Stella Thomas, whom I visited often as a child when my family made the trek to Flippin, Arkansas every year from New Mexico. Grandma and grandpa Thomas lived in Flippin during the early 60's while Aunt Minnie lived alone in Plainview, Texas in a neat and orderly assisted living apartment. She always had her special Jell-O and cookies waiting whenever I had the honor of sharing her company.

1 can dark bing cherries (pitted)
1 (6oz) pkg dark cherry Jell-O
1 box Dream Whip (2 pkgs)

Drain cherries in colander saving cherry juice in a measuring cup. Cut cherries into fourths and set aside. Dissolve Jell-O in an amount of hot water, which when added to the cherry juice, will make a total of 2 cups of liquid. Add Jell-O mixture to the juice and chill until partially set. Add cherries and beat with mixer. Chill in a 9 1/2x11-inch pan. Prepare Dream Whip according to package directions. When Jell-O mixture is well set, beat in Dream Whip. Chill until ready to serve.

Lime-Marshmallow-Pineapple Salad

Barbara Linde, Ph.D.

This is a great recipe for parties. I usually garnish with part of the Jell-O. Pour a little of the Jell-O in a pan and when it jells, cut out bells or hearts or any design and place over the chilled salad. FUN!

1 sm pkg lime Jell-O	1 cup hot water
3 cups miniature marshmallows	1 cup cold water
1 tsp mayonnaise (rounded)	1 cup whipped cream
1 sm can pineapple (undrained)	
1 (8 oz) pkg cream cheese (softened)	

Dissolve the gelatin in 1 cup of hot water. Add cream cheese, blending in well; then add marshmallows, stirring until the marshmallows are soft. Add the cup of cold water. Chill until syrupy; then add whipped cream (or Dream Whip), mayonnaise and pineapple with juice. Blend well and chill until firm.

Note: I have used one package of Dream Whip for the whipped cream. I have also used other flavors of gelatin – for the different seasons of the year - red strawberry or cherry for February holidays, orange for October or November holidays, etc.

Cranberry Salad

Theresa M. Baldridge

This recipe was given to me by a very special person in my life, Ethel Lipscomb. Ethel is now in a nursing home and can no longer cook for family and friends.

2 cans whole cranberry sauce
2 cups frozen strawberries
1/2 cup pecans (chopped)
1 (20 oz) can crushed pineapple (drained)

Drain strawberries and reserve juice. Mix all ingredients together. If too dry, add some of the strawberry juice. Place in refrigerator to chill. May also be frozen and served after thawing.

Sauerkraut Salad

Joanne Berger

I got this recipe from a dear lady I met in Hill City, South Dakota. Her name was June Clines. She and her daughter, Dianne Murray, had a lovely gift shop. We vacationed in South Dakota for several years in the 70's and became friends. We kept in touch by mail and shared many recipes over the years.

1 large can sauerkraut
1 jar pimiento
3 tbsp vinegar

1 green pepper
1 cup sugar

Drain sauerkraut, add chopped green pepper and drained pimiento. Mix sugar and vinegar together and pour over sauerkraut mixture. Stir well.

Spinach and Strawberry Salad

Judy Martin

4 cups sliced strawberries
1/2 cup vegetable oil
1/4 cup white wine vinegar
1/4 tsp paprika
2 bunches of spinach (rinsed and torn into bite-size pieces)

2 tbsp sesame seeds
1 tbsp poppy seeds
1/2 cup sugar

In a large bowl, combine spinach and strawberries. In a medium-sized bowl, whisk together the oil, vinegar, sugar, paprika, sesame seeds and poppy seeds. Pour over salad, toss well until mixed and serve.

Deer Chili

John Sowells

1/2 lb deer meat
2 cans of tomatoes (diced)
1 onion (diced)
1 lg can of tomato juice
chili powder to taste

1/2 lb sausage (your favorite)
2 cans of mushroom pieces
1 bell pepper (diced)
your favorite seasonings

Cook deer meat and sausages thoroughly. In a large bowl, mix the remaining ingredients together. In a large stew pot, combine cooked meet and all other ingredients. Cook on medium heat for 1 hour.

Microwave Chili

Pam Hurst

1 lb ground beef (lean)
2 (8 oz) cans tomato sauce
1 pkg McCormick's original chili seasoning
1 (15 oz) can kidney or pinto beans (undrained)
water (8 oz) optional

Brown beef, drain excess fat from the pan. In microwave-safe large covered dish, combine beef and seasoning mix. Stir in tomato sauce, undrained beans and water (optional). Microwave on high power for 6 minutes. Stir thoroughly. Microwave for an additional 6 minutes on high power or until desired temperature. Makes 4 servings.

Polska Soup

Marilyn (Graham) Cunningham
Flippin High School Graduate, 1962

I created this recipe from a soup that I had eaten at The Olive Garden restaurant. The Polska soup is quick, easy and good! It is great for cold, wintry days.

6–8 medium red potatoes
1 pkg Polska Kielbasa
3 tbsp butter

1/2 white onion
1/2 cup half-n-half
salt and pepper

Chop potatoes and onion. Boil until tender. Lower heat. Skin and slice Kielbasa. Cut slices in half. Add to potatoes and onions. Cook on low heat for 15 minutes. Add half-n-half and butter and season with salt and pepper to taste. Serve with crackers, croutons or hot buttery corn bread. Makes 6-8 cups.

Salad Dressing Tips

When tossing a salad with a basic vinaigrette, always make the vinaigrette at least 1/2 hour ahead of time and let the mixture sit to allow the flavors to marry. Pour the vinaigrette down the side of the bowl, not directly on the greens, for a more evenly dressed salad.

Vegetable Soup for Two   Jean Bourne

1/2 carrot (grated)   1 cup chicken broth, divided
2 tbsp green pepper (chopped)
3/4 tsp sugar   1 tbsp onion (chopped)
3/4 tsp pepper   1 tbsp butter
1 tbsp flour
1/2 celery rib (chopped)
1 (14 1/2 oz) can tomatoes (diced)

Sauté carrots, celery, green pepper and onion until tender. Add tomatoes, sugar, pepper and broth (reserve 2 tablespoons of broth). Simmer for 10 minutes. Combine flour and 2 tablespoons broth. Add to soup and cook for 2 additional minutes. Makes 2 servings.

Taco Soup   Carole Rietveld

I garnish this soup with sour cream, chopped green onions, chopped tomatoes, grated cheese and black olive slices. The flavors are even better the second day! I make double and quadruple batches, divide into gallon sized freezer bags and have it on hand for quick, delicious meals and for unexpected guests. Enjoy and share with friends!

1 1/2 lb lean hamburger   1 medium onion (chopped)
1 (28 oz) can diced tomatoes 1 (16 oz) can pinto beans
1 (16 oz) can black beans   1 (16 oz) red kidney beans
1 cup water   1 pkg taco seasoning mix
1 (16 oz) can whole kernel corn
1 (16 oz) can tomato sauce

Brown hamburger and onions in a large kettle. Add remaining ingredients. Simmer for 30 minutes. Serve with tortilla chips.

> If a soup or stew is too salty, add raw cut potatoes. Discard them after they have cooked - they will have absorbed the salt.

SIDE DISHES

Flippin's Rugged Years

During the 1930's through the 50's Marion County was then "wet" (liquor was legal), gambling was legal, and with the influx of so many new people from all walks of life moving into the county, sometimes things got a little out of hand. Numerous fights and several killings helped to gain Flippin a reputation as being a fairly tough town.

Flippin had several taverns. One tavern, The Silver Star Night Club was considered a real "honky-tonk" and was located where the Ranger Boats Company sits today. Dances and dance marathons were common. The Silver Star tavern, and the jail house in Flippin, were seldom empty on a Friday or Saturday night.

After the Bull Shoals Dam was completed in 1952, citizens voted to "dry up" Marion County. The Silver Star Night Club was purchased by several business men for industrial use. Even years after it's closing, some locals say they could still hear its music on a quiet night.

Several years later, Forrest Wood purchased the old wood frame Silver Star building and modestly began to build the empire that is Ranger Boats today. The building burned to the ground on May 4, 1971, in one of the most infamous fires in Flippin history.

The historic Old Flippin City Jail (circa 1920) still stands on Second Street, in Flippin, Arkansas

Forrest and Nina Wood

Founders of Ranger Boats, Flippin, Arkansas

High school sweethearts, Forrest and Nina forged a lifelong bond very early in their lives. Both came from backgrounds of simple beginnings and lots of hard work. They applied what they learned young in life to a business partnership that began with jobs such as raising cattle, contractor services, and operating a successful fishing guide service on Bull Shoals Lake, the White and Buffalo Rivers and Crooked Creek.

In 1968, Forrest's long hours and years of guiding had taught him the value and real need for a boat which was comfortable, efficient, and of good quality. With those merits in mind, and a need for an income in the winter months, his dream to build a quality fishing boat began.

It was the time when bass tournaments were starting up in earnest in the Southeast so what he started out making was what Forrest described as a lake boat. Forrest decided to attend one of the fishing tournaments on Greers Ferry Lake to find out if anyone was interested in buying boats from him. One of those boats he sold was to Bill Dance, who went on to become a legend on the pro-fishing circuit.

The original six Ranger boats were built in 1968 in what is now the Fire House in downtown Flippin, Arkansas. Soon afterward, manufacturing was moved to an unoccupied dance hall, The Silver Star. On May 4, 1971, one of the most infamous fires in Flippin history burned down the Ranger Boats factory. Bound and determined to keep his 60 employees on the payroll, Forrest nailed a phone to a tree near the ruins of the plant and began to conduct business while friends helped clean up the rubble. Sixty boat orders were salvaged from an army surplus desk. A new manufacturing plant was rebuilt on the same site and exactly 40 days later began making boats again.

Anyone who is closely associated with Ranger Boats will point to Wood and his wife, Nina, as the cornerstones of the company. A large percentage of workers at Ranger Boats are local Flippin residents who started out 10, 20 or even 30 years ago and are there today.

Forrest and Nina are well established in the forefront of the sport fishing industry with Forrest as the namesake of the premier Wal-Mart FLW tournaments, with seven national tournament circuits offering a combined $36.5 million in awards through 235 events in 2005.

In 1998 Forrest was awarded the honor of being the first Marion County resident to be appointed to the Arkansas Game and Fish Commission by Arkansas Governor Mike Huckabee.

In 2004 the Forrest L. Wood Crowley's Ridge Nature Center in Jonesboro, Arkansas was named in honor of Forrest Wood. It covers some 160 acres, including about 100 acres of woodlands. It is the second of four such Arkansas Game and Fish educational facilities planned in the state.

In 2005 the Arkansas Game and Fish Commission's Rivercliff Access in Marion County was renamed to honor the Woods as the Forrest and Nina Wood State Park Access. J.A. and Nancy Morgan, ancestors of Nina (Kirkland) Wood, homesteaded the site of the access. Her maternal grandparents, Jim and Mattie (Morgan) Swan and her parents, Floyd and Myrtle (Swan) Kirkland farmed the land prior to the Bull Shoals dam's construction. Forrest and Nina owned and operated the State Park Boat Dock and a float trip service at the site in the late 1960's.

Forrest and Nina live in Flippin, Arkansas and have four daughters: Brenda Hopper, Linda Daffron, Rhonda Layton, and Donna Alexander as well as eleven grandchildren and eight great-grandchildren.

Forrest and Nina Wood

Potato Casserole

Myrt Flippin

(12 oz) grated cheddar cheese
1 (8oz) pkg sour cream
2 cup corn flakes (crushed)
1 can cream of chicken soup
1 pkg shredded frozen potatoes (I like to use O'Brien shredded hash browns with onions and peppers)

1/4 cup butter
1/4 cup butter (melted)
1 tsp salt

Put thawed potatoes in a 9x13-inch dish. Mix with sour cream, salt, soup and cheese. Top with cornflakes. Pour melted butter over top and bake uncovered at 350° F degrees for 45 minutes.

Green Bean Casserole

John Sowells

4 cans french style green beans
1 can cream of mushroom soup
1 can cream of celery soup
1 onion (diced)
1 can mushroom pieces (undrained)
1 can french fried onions
shredded cheese for topping

Mix beans, soups, onion and mushrooms together in a casserole dish. Top with shredded cheese and French fried onions. Cover and bake at 300° F for 1 hour.

Crock Pot Corn

Michella Seawright

1 (32 oz or 48 oz) bag frozen corn
3/4 cup sugar
1 stick butter
salt & pepper to taste
1 (8oz) pkg Philadelphia cream cheese

Layer in crock pot corn, sugar, butter, cream cheese, salt and pepper. Mix when hot. Let SLOW cook for about 4 hours.

Sweet Potato Casserole

Linda Swaters

2 eggs
1 stick margarine or butter
1 tsp vanilla extract
3 cups sweet potatoes (peeled, cooked and mashed, approx 6 potatoes)

1 cup sugar
1/2 cup milk

Topping:
1 cup brown sugar
1/3 cup flour

1/4 cup margarine
1 cup pecans (chopped)

Mash cooked sweet potatoes while still hot. Add butter so it will melt. Set aside. Beat eggs and sugar, add milk and vanilla. Gradually add mixture to sweet potatoes. Place in a greased 2-quart baking dish. To make topping, mix brown sugar, flour and margarine with your fingers! Make fine crumbs. Sprinkle over sweet potatoes. Cover with nuts and bake at 350° F for 30–45 minutes.

Broccoli Casserole

Brenda Young

This was first brought to a family dinner and now is at every family dinner. Even people that don't like broccoli like this!

2 pkg frozen chopped broccoli
1 can cream of celery soup
1/2 stick butter or margarine (sliced)
1/2 lb Velveeta cheese
1 sleeve Ritz crackers (crumbled)

Cook broccoli as directed on package, then drain. Layer the ingredients, broccoli, butter, celery soup, Velveeta and crackers into a 2 quart baking dish. Bake in moderate oven at 350° F until bubbles appear, approximately 30 minutes.

Green Rice Casserole

Linda Swaters

1/4 cup oil
1 cup milk
2 eggs (beaten)
1 1/2 lb Velveeta cheese (cut into small cubes)
1 pkg frozen broccoli (thawed and chopped)
1 1/2 cups minute rice (1 box for 6 servings – cooked)

Mix all ingredients well. Bake at 350° F for 1 hour in an oven-safe casserole dish.

Green Rice

Mary M. Ritter, Roslinda M. Wells, Quarry Mountain Ranch LLC

This recipe is submitted in memory of our aunt, Eunice Lenox Wilson, who prepared it often when we came to visit her and our uncle, Johnnie P. Wilson. It's best made up in the morning and let stand until ready to bake.

2 cups cooked rice
2 cups milk
2 eggs
1/2 cup vegetable oil
1 (2 oz) jar chopped pimiento
salt, pepper & Tabasco to taste

1 medium onion (chopped)
2 tbsp parsley flakes
2 cloves garlic (chopped)
1/4 lb Velveeta cheese

Combine all ingredients, place in a greased oven-proof dish. Bake at 350° F until set – about 1 hour. Makes 6 servings. Freezes well.

Three stalks of celery, chopped and added to about two cups of beans (navy, brown, pinto, etc), will make them easier to digest.

One Pot Chili Beans

Myrt Flippin

Letting this slow cook makes it even tastier!

1 lb pinto beans
2 lb lean ground beef
1 onion (chopped)

2 tsp salt
2 cloves garlic
2 tbsp chili powder

Combine all ingredients in a big pot. Add enough water to barely cover. Bring to a boil and simmer until the beans are bursting (about 2 1/2 hours).

White Beans

Lee Powell

A friend of mine, here in Arkansas, would like a side of these beans at almost every meal!

2 carrots (shredded)
1 onion (finely diced)
3 celery stalks (diced finely)
1 pkg great northern beans (soaked in water overnight)

After soaking beans overnight, rinse and put in crock pot. Cover with water. Add vegetables, salt and black pepper. Cover and cook on the high setting for 8-10 hours, stirring occasionally, until beans are soft and juice is thickened.

Ozark Lima Beans

Jennie Ply

1/4 cup of butter or margarine
1/4 cup onion (chopped)
1 (8 oz) can of mushrooms (drained)
2 (10 oz) pkg frozen lima beans (cooked and drained)
2 chicken bouillon cubes (dissolved in 1 cup of boiling water)

2 tbsp parsley (chopped)
2 tbsp flour

Preheat oven to 350° F. Place beans in 2 quart casserole. Set aside. Saute parsley and onion in butter in small pan. Remove from heat and stir in flour. Add chicken bouillon and mix well. Add mushrooms. Pour sauce over beans. Bake 20-30 minutes or until bubbly. Serves 8.

Okra Patties

Doris Merrill

2 cups okra (sliced thin)   2 cups self-rising corn meal
1/2 cup onion (chopped)   1/2 cup bell pepper (chopped)
1 tsp salt   dash of black pepper
1 1/2 - 2 cups canned tomatoes
bacon drippings for frying

Mix the okra, corn meal, onion, pepper, salt and black pepper in a bowl. Add the tomatoes to this mixture; mix well. Form the mixture into thin patties. Place into a hot skillet with bacon drippings. Cook slowly until brown on both sides. Use just enough drippings to cook good and keep from burning.

Okra Side

Lee Powell

This is truly a southern side dish. I moved to the Ozarks from Chicago, Illinois. A friend of mine, born and raised in Arkansas, gave me this recipe.

1 large pkg frozen breaded okra
   (fried crisp, drained on paper towels and set on side)
8 pieces bacon
   (fried crisp, drained on paper towel and crumbled)
2 tomatoes (chopped into tiny bite sized pieces)
1 bell pepper (chopped into tiny bite sized pieces)
1 bunch green onions (chopped into tiny bite sized pieces)

Dressing:
1/2 cup sugar or Splenda,
1/4 cup canola or vegetable oil
1/8 cup white vinegar

Fry okra and bacon, set aside to drain and cool. Mix dressing ingredients together. When ready to serve, mix okra, bacon and vegetables together. Toss with dressing.

Rice Dressing
Vera Bockelman

1 cup rice (cooked and drained)	1 tbsp butter
1/2 cup celery (chopped)	1 onion (chopped)
1 lb pork sausage	2 eggs
1 tsp sage	salt & pepper to taste

Sauté celery and onion until tender. Add to the cooked rice and pork sausage. Beat eggs slightly. Mix in eggs, sage, salt and pepper to taste to the mixture and stuff in your favorite bird. Cook inside the bird or in a casserole dish in your oven.

> For fluffier, whiter rice, add one teaspoon of lemon juice per litre (quart) of water. To add extra flavour and nutrition to rice, cook it in liquid reserved from cooking vegetables.

Southern Cornbread Dressing
Linda Swaters

3 cups cornbread (crumbled)	2-3 eggs
4-5 cups turkey or chicken stock	1/2 cup melted butter
1 onion (chopped fine)	1/2 tsp salt
1/4 cup celery (finely chopped)	1/2 tsp pepper
6 tbsp sage	
2 1/2 cups day-old, dry, light bread (crumbled)	

Mix breads, add raw eggs and other ingredients, mixing thoroughly. Dressing should be soft, about the consistency of cake batter. (This is the secret of good dressing because it will bake dry). Bake in greased 9x13-inch baking dish at 425° F for about 40 minutes. Serves 10 -12.

Note: If you wish, you may stuff the turkey with this dressing. Roast the bird at 325° F and allow 5 minutes more cooking time per pound than you would for an unstuffed bird.

Baked Corn Dish
Edith Williams

1 can whole kernel corn
1/2 cup oleo margarine
1 cup sour cream
1 (8 1/2 oz) pkg corn bread mix
1 cup shredded cheese

1 can creamy style corn
1 egg (beaten)
1/2 tsp salt

Partly drain the whole kernel corn; add creamy style corn, oleo, sour cream, egg, salt and corn bread mix. Put into 9x13-inch baking pan. Bake at 350° F for 30 minutes. Remove from oven and put shredded cheese on top. Return to oven for 10 –15 additional minutes until cheese is melted.

Hush Puppies
Jennie Ply

1 cup flour (self rising)
1/8 tsp salt
1 egg
1 med onion (chopped)
1 1/2 cups buttermilk — or as needed

1 cup cornmeal
1/4 tsp baking soda
fat — for deep frying

Sift together flour, cornmeal, salt, and soda. Add egg and buttermilk until it's the right consistency to hold its shape when rolled into a ball. Mix in onion, then roll into balls about 1-2 inches across and drop in deep hot fat. Fry until they're brown and crispy. Let them drain a bit on some paper and serve hot. Serves 10

Vinegar And Cucumbers
Dottie Osmundson

1 cup vinegar
1 cup water
2/3 cup sugar
1/2 tsp salt

dash of pepper
2 large cucumbers
1 slice white onion

Mix together vinegar, water, sugar, salt and pepper in bowl. Slice in cucumbers. Add slice of onion. This can be served immediately or refrigerated to serve later. Serves 5 to 6 people.

Fried Cornmeal Cakes

Connie Ply

This recipe came to me from my mother's mother. Granny Morrison was half Native American. Her mother was an Indian Princess which meant my great grandmother was a chief's daughter. But you could rarely get Granny to talk about her heritage because she was raised at a time in history when being even half Native American was worse than being a stray dog. Granny was very self-sufficient. At 78 years of age, when she got ready for a "mess" (her term) of squirrel or rabbit, she would take her gun and go hunting. She always came back with the game. She was an amazing woman and I'm very proud to be her granddaughter!

1 1/2 cups cornmeal	1/2 cup flour
1 egg (lightly beaten)	1/4 cup water
3/4 cup buttermilk	
1/2 small yellow onion (diced)	
1/2 cup whole kernel corn (drained)	

In a medium sized bowl, mix cornmeal, flour and diced onion. Add egg, buttermilk and water. Mix well. This should make a thick dough. If mixture is too thick, continue adding water until mixture is easy to stir. Add corn and mix well. Heat skillet on medium heat with just enough oil to coat the bottom of the skillet. The pan is ready when a drop of water will dance across the bottom of the skillet when dropped into it. Spoon enough mixture into the skillet to make a medium sized oval (similar in size to a medium sized pancake). Let cook until bubbles appear on top of the oval. Flip with a pancake turner. Let cook until golden brown. Remove from skillet. Top with butter or margarine if desired. Repeat process until all mixture is gone. Serve with a glass of cold milk, but they are even better with buttermilk!

Grits and Cheese Bake
William (Bill) Hunter

I was born and raised in Montréal Quebec Canada. I traveled the world over in Canada, USA and Europe working as an international sales contract manager for a British manufacturer of medical supplies. I never heard about grits until I came south. Here is about the only way I'll eat grits!

1 tsp salt	2 eggs (well beaten)
4 cups boiling water	1/2 cup milk
1/2 cup butter or margarine	
1/2 cup parmesan cheese (grated)	
1 1/2 (6oz) cups cheddar cheese (shredded)	
1 cup enriched white hominy quick grits	

Stir grits slowly into salted boiling water in large heavy saucepan. Cook over low heat for about 5 minutes, stirring occasionally. Stir in cheddar cheese, 1/4 cup parmesan cheese, butter, milk and eggs. Continue cooking over low heat until cheddar cheese is melted. Pour into greased 1 1/2 quart casserole; sprinkle with remaining parmesan cheese. Bake in a preheated 350° F oven for 1 hour. Makes 6 servings.

Broccoli Bake
Joanne Berger

My daughter Janice, and I would have this dish for our supper and there were never any leftovers. She didn't like plain vegetables but really liked this dish.

1 can cream of mushroom soup	1/2 cup bread crumbs
1/2 cup milk	2 tbsp butter (melted)
1/2 cup mayonnaise	2 eggs (beaten)
2 pkg frozen broccoli spears	
1 cup (4 oz) cheddar cheese (shredded)	

Cook broccoli in salted water 10–12 minutes until barely tender. Drain. Place in an 8x12-inch pan. In a separate bowl combine soup, milk, cheese, mayonnaise and the beaten eggs. Pour over broccoli. Combine bread crumbs and melted butter. Sprinkle on top. Bake at 350° F for 35 minutes.

Taters, Eggs and Cheese   Niellein Stice

When there's not much in the frig to eat, you learn to put what there is together to make a meal. That's what we did – it's wonderful!

6 eggs
1 small onion
1 pinch of salt
salsa to taste
6–8 potatoes (taters)
garlic powder to taste

1 pinch of pepper
1 cup cheddar cheese
6 slices of bacon

Fry up diced taters (potatoes) with diced onions, salt, pepper and garlic powder until done. Fry up bacon, set aside. In a bowl, whip up eggs, pour over top of taters. Lower heat and cover. When eggs are done, cover top with grated cheese and crumbled bacon. Serve with salsa.

Perfect Mashed Potatoes   Lee Powell

My grandmother perfected this recipe for my grandfather.

2 tbsp butter
1/2 cup (more or less) cream
1/2 cup of sour cream
3-4 Potatoes (about 1 pound, pared and diced)

Boil potatoes in salted water, until soft when pierced with fork. Drain and return potatoes to pot. Add butter, cream and sour cream. Mash all together, add salt and pepper to taste, beat with an electric mixer until light and fluffy.

To make lighter and fluffier mashed potatoes, add a pinch or two of baking powder to the potatoes before whipping.

Poke Salat

Betty Burnett

My husband, Dean, son Mike, and I moved from Kansas City to Everton, Arkansas in 1955. My younger son, David was born during the time we lived on the farm. We then relocated to Mountain Home, Arkansas and lived there for several years. In 1998 we built a log home in Flippin, Arkansas. We love our log home and enjoy raising a vegetable garden, flowers and trying to keep the deer and "critters" from eating everything!

poke weed   cooked bacon, chopped or bacon grease
salt & pepper

Gather a mess of poke. Clean and wash. Put in large pot and cover with water. Bring to a boil. Cook until poke is tender. Drain and rinse poke (Very Important!). Put poke back in pot and add some water. Add some salt, pepper and some chopped cooked bacon or bacon grease. Bring back to boil and serve.

Potatoes and Carrots

Violet Hensley

Here's a recipe I cooked up back in 1940 when I had to mix potatoes and carrots to have a meal. We liked it so much I've cooked it ever since.

4 medium potatoes (sliced thin, for frying)
1 small onion (chopped)
2 medium carrots (peeled, sliced very thin)
1 tsp salt

Slice carrots thinner than potatoes, as the potatoes cook faster. Mix and fry all as you would when frying only a skillet of potatoes. I let mine fry until lightly browned, then turn and fry a little more. I then place the lid on and steam for a few minutes more. Takes 7-8 minutes to cook.

MAIN DISHES & STEWS

"Industry Come Here!"

"Industry Come Here!" was the civic cry of Flippin residents after a city water tank had been erected.

In 1955, Flippin did not have a water system. After losing negotiations with a clothing manufacturing plant to Cotter, the residents were awakened to the fact that in order to progress, the town must have a water and fire protection system.

An improvement district was formed and plans got underway for "city water". An 800 foot well was drilled with a flow of 60 gallons of water per minute. A 100,000 gallon water tank was acquired and water lines and fire hydrants were installed.

Early in December, 1956, Mabel Stucks used the first Flippin city water. Originally 100 water meters and 9 fire hydrants were installed.

In 1956 twenty residences installed new bathrooms, mostly since the new water system was installed.

The Sanders Family

A Long Tradition of Serving the Community

When the name "Sanders," come to mind, you automatically think of Marion County frontier settlers, as the Sanders family moved to this area in the early 1850's, nearly 150-years ago.

The Tom Sanders family came by covered wagon from Tennessee and settled on a farm on Jimmies Creek near the Wild Cat Ford. Tom Sanders brought along with him a number of slaves, probably three or four, according to a volume of Marion County History.

Sanders & Son Grocery in 2006

When the Civil War broke out, Tom freed his slaves, prior to the Emancipation Proclamation and joined the Confederate Army. These former slaves chose to live on the farm, and work during the Civil War, and some of them were buried in the Wild Cat Cemetery.

When Tom and Peggy Sanders came to these parts in the middle 1800's, they pitched their camps and built their fires, probably not realizing the impact of their move as many offspring's continue to live in the immediate area. The daughter of Shane Sanders, Shannon, is the seventh-generation of Sanders to live in Marion County. Tom and Peggy are buried in the Fairview Cemetery.

The Great-great-grandchildren of Tom Sanders, Chuck and Jimmy, (brothers) both have businesses on Main Street in Flippin and this is something that their dad, R.D. Sanders took a lot of pride in telling people about. The family Sanders & Son's Grocery store started in 1936 by L.O. and R.D Sanders (father and son) was then known as Sanders General Merchandise store. The store
64

originated in the Parnell building, offering dry goods, clothing, feed, tack, horseshoes and just about anything you would expect in a general merchandise store. In 1942 they relocated the business when they bought the Cornell building and moved it to it's present location. A refrigerated meat case was added in 1948, a rarity for a small town at the time. After a remodel in 1957, the general merchandise was phased out. Today Sander's and Sons is run by Chuck and Kathy's son, Shane, a fourth-generation grocery owner in the same building!

The Cornell building

Jimmy has his own State Farm Insurance Agency. Jimmy was born in Flippin in 1944 and graduated from Flippin High School in 1962. He entered the grocery business with his dad and his brother Chuck, thus becoming the third-generation Sanders to carry on the family grocery business in Flippin. In 1966, he enrolled in college at the University of Arkansas, in Fayetteville where he majored in Physical Education and received his BSE Degree in just 34-months. Jimmy related how he left for college with $400.00 in his pockets and a desire to succeed at what he was doing. Arriving in Fayetteville, he began his studies during the day and worked at a Fire Department at night as an ambulance driver and rescue personnel, receiving a salary and room accommodations at the department.

It is clear to see how the work ethic and courage of Tom and Peggy Sanders set the tone for all the generations of Sanders that followed. The Sanders family has been a Flippin landmark since the 1800's. When you come for a visit to Flippin, be sure to visit Main Street and stop by the Sanders & Son's Grocery Store and the State Farm Insurance office to say 'howdy' to Chuck and Jimmy Sanders!

Fried Frog Connie Ply

The story behind this recipe is probably more interesting than the recipe itself! When we lived in Iowa (1958-1968) a full blooded Cherokee Indian named Dewey Greyton and his wife Mary lived next door to us. As young girls, my sister and I loved to hear the stories that Dewey and Mary told of life on the reservation. They taught us to frog gig; wading chest deep in the Mississippi River, carrying a tow sack. Now folks we are talking about good sized bull frogs! Dewey taught us how to clean the frogs and use everything but the head, feet and guts. This consisted of a lot of pumping of the pump handle on the well! We lost track of Dewey and Mary after we moved back to Arkansas in 1968. But Dewey taught me to be proud of and to respect my Native American heritage. Dewey and Mary, if you are still alive and this somehow reaches you – Thank You for the love, understanding and wonderful memories you gave this "little" girl. You both have a special place in my heart.

1 cup flour	1 tbsp salt
1 tbsp pepper	cayenne pepper to taste
1 can evaporated milk	1 large egg

several bull frogs (cleaned, soaking in salt water
   – this keeps them from "jumping" out of the frying pan)

Drain salt water from frogs and rinse well under cold running water. Drain. Heat a cast iron skillet with 1/4 inch cooking oil over medium heat. (You know oil is hot enough when a drop of water in the oil sizzles. Keep the oil this hot). Mix flour, salt and pepper together. Mix evaporated milk and beaten egg together in a separate bowl. Dip frog into milk and egg mixture. Drain off excess. Roll frog in flour. Place in frying pan. Turn when 1 side is golden brown. Continue this process until all frogs are fried.

> Drain deep fried foods on brown paper grocery bags as opposed to paper towels to retain crispness.

Squirrel & Dumplings

Karen Shelby

Serve with a side of green beans and a skillet of hot cornbread.

2 squirrels (cleaned and quartered)
2 cans chicken broth
1 large onion (coarsely chopped)
1 stalk celery (diced)
2 cloves garlic (minced)
1 qt of water
1 bay leaf
salt and pepper to taste

Dumplings:
1 1/2 cup baking mix (such as Bisquick®)
1 tsp black pepper
1 tsp parsley flakes
1/2 cup water

In a large heavy sauce pan add the squirrels, onion, garlic, celery, broth and bay leaf, bring to a boil then simmer for about 45 minutes. Remove squirrel from liquid (let cool so you can handle) and debone, returning meat to broth. Salt and pepper to taste. Discard the bay leaf. Bring broth mixture to a low boil. In the mean time, place the baking mix, black pepper and parsley flakes in a bowl and stir. Add the water and mix. This mixture should be stiff but not flaky, you can add more baking mix or water by spoonfuls until desired consistency is reached.

Drop the dumpling mixture into the boiling broth by teaspoonfuls. Reduce heat, cover and simmer for about 10 minutes. The dumplings will thicken the broth, they will rise and get fluffy on the inside, like biscuits.

> To deodorize a plastic storage container in which onions or garlic were stored, wash thoroughly, then stuff a crumpled piece of newspaper in the container, and snap on the lid. In a few days the smell will disappear.

Fried Squirrel

Connie Ply

This recipe came to me from my Granny Davis, my daddy's mother. This recipe probably is an Ozark's original as my Granny was a Kirkendol by birth. Her family and two other families pioneered the land that is now Clinton, Arkansas and the surrounding areas.

4-6 squirrels (cleaned and washed)
1 1/2 cups plain flour
1 dash cayenne pepper
1 dash of garlic powder
1 dash dried orange peel

1 tbsp salt
1 1/2 tsp black pepper
1 dash lemon peel (dried)
2 eggs

Soak squirrels for 30 minutes in cold salt water. Mix all dry ingredients together in a bowl or plastic bag. Drain salt water from meat and rinse in cold running water. Beat eggs in small bowl and dip each piece of squirrel in egg mixture. Let excess egg drain off meat. Coat with flour mixture. Place in cast iron skillet in 1 inch of cooking oil at medium heat. Fry slowly, turning each piece as needed until done.

Hunter's Delight

Jane Herbst

6 pork chops (browned)
1 onion (chopped)
1 tsp oregano
1 can mushrooms (drained)
1 cup minute rice, uncooked
1 can cream of mushroom soup

1 cup celery (chopped)
1 green pepper (chopped)
1/2 tsp salt & pepper
1 soup can of milk

Combine all ingredients and pour over pork chops. Bake uncovered for 30 minutes at 350 ° F .

Marinating is a cinch if you use a plastic bag. The meat stays in the marinade and it's easy to turn and rearrange. Cleanup is easy too; just toss the bag.

Squirrel and Dumplings

Betty Burnett

This dish is good with rice!

2 squirrels
1 medium onion
3 slices of bacon (uncooked)

water to cover
1 pinch of salt
1 can biscuits

First, you shoot a couple of squirrels. Skin and gut them. Put the cleaned squirrels in a pot and cover with water. Add some onion, salt, bacon or bacon grease. Bring to a boil and simmer until squirrel is tender., about 45 minutes. Remove squirrels and let cool. Debone the squirrels and put the meat back into the pot. Bring back to a boil again. Open a can of biscuits and cut each biscuit into fourths. Place biscuit pieces on surface and cover with lid. Simmer covered for 10 minutes or until the biscuits are cooked. Thicken broth with cornstarch mixed with water and serve.

Indian Lamb Curry

Jodi Takhar

This Indian dish is very flavorful. Serve with Naan bread.

2 lb lamb (cut in about 2 inch pieces)
1 black cardamom pod, (ground up or use ground cardamom)
1/4 + 1/16 tsp cinnamon
7 whole cloves
1/2 tsp garlic paste (comes in a jar)
1 1/4 tsp turmeric
1 1/4 tsp curry powder
2 tsp (heaping) tomato paste
6 onions (peeled, minced fine or grated)
salt to taste

Mix together in crock pot onions, lamb, cardamom, cinnamon and cloves. Cook on high for 1 1/2 hours. Mix together in a bowl, garlic paste, turmeric, curry powder and tomato paste. Mix into crock pot. Cook on high for approximatley 2 1/2 hours until meat is tender. Add water as needed, if liquid boils away. Serve with basmati rice and plain yogurt. Serves 4-5.

Substitution: Beef roast instead of lamb

Moroccan Venison With Rice   Karen Shelby

2 cups beef broth   2 tbsp olive oil
1 1/2 tsp ground ginger   1 tsp salt
1/2 tsp black pepper   1 lemon (thinly sliced)
3 cups hot cooked rice
3 large tomatoes (coarsely chopped)
2 large onions (chopped, about 2 cups)
1/8 tsp ground red pepper (cayenne, optional)
12 cloves garlic (whole, yes, I said 12 cloves)
1/3 cup chopped fresh parsley (2 tablespoons dried)
1/2 cup chopped fresh coriander leaves or (3 tablespoons dried)
1 1/2 pounds venison roast (cut into 1-inch cubes, can substitute beef)

In a large bowl, mix all ingredients except the rice and pour in an ungreased 3-quart casserole. Cover and bake 2 1/2 to 3 hours at 325° F or until venison is very tender. Serve over hot cooked rice with tomato, cucumber and apple salad. (See page 44 for recipe).

Lamb with Apples and Raisins   Dottie Osmundson

2 tbsp butter   1 medium onion (peeled and diced)
1 clove garlic (minced) 2 tsp curry powder
1/4 tsp ground ginger   1/4 cup raisins
1 chicken bullion cube   2 cups lamb (diced and cooked)
1 cup water   2 tsp lemon juice
1 large tart apple (unpeeled, cored and diced)

In a skillet cook onion in butter until limp. Stir in garlic. Add apple, curry, ginger, raisins, bullion, lamb and water. Mix together and simmer for 10 minutes. Blend 1 teaspoon cornstarch in 1 teaspoon water and stir into lamb mixture. Cook until thickened. Remove from heat and stir in lemon juice. Serve over basmati rice. Serves 2.

Roast Opossum

The opossum is a very fat animal with a peculiarly flavored meat.

1 opossum (dressed and washed)
Dressing:

1 lg onion (minced)	1 sweet red pepper (chopped
1 tbsp fat	dash Worcestershire sauce
opossum liver (chopped)	1 egg (cooked hard, chopped)
1 cup bread crumbs	salt

Brown the onion in the fat. Add liver and cook until liver is tender. Add bread crumbs and red pepper, Worcestershire sauce, egg, salt and water to moisten. Stuff opossum and place in roaster. Add 2 tablespoons of water and roast at 350° F for 1-1 1/2 hours. Baste every 15 minutes with drippings. Skim fat from pan gravy. Serve gravy separately, with baked yams or sweet potatoes. Serves 10.

Quail In Onion Gravy   Karen Shelby

8-10 quail (cleaned and dressed)	salt & pepper to taste
8 slices bacon	1 clove garlic (minced)
1 cup cooking oil	1 medium onion (sliced)
1 cup chicken broth	
3/4 cup flour, divided (all-purpose)	

Sprinkle quail with salt and pepper, dredge in ½ cup flour, set aside. In a large Dutch oven, fry the bacon until done. Remove the bacon from the Dutch oven, drain on paper towels. Crumble and set aside. Add cooking oil to the Dutch oven and heat over medium heat. Add the quail and cook 10-12 minutes on each side or until done. Remove quail and drain on paper towels. Remove drippings from Dutch oven, reserving ¼ cup in Dutch oven. Add 1/4 cup flour to drippings, stirring until combined and smooth. Cook 1 minute. Gradually add the chicken broth, stirring constantly. Add the onion and garlic and cook over medium heat, stirring constantly, until thick and bubbly and the onion is tender. Salt and pepper to taste. To serve, place 2 quail on a bed of wild rice and pour onion gravy over the top.

Spanish Rice with Beef   Gail Flippin

This is a quick dish to prepare and very tasty

3/4 lb ground beef	1/2 tsp chili powder
1 pkg (10 oz) frozen corn	1/2 tsp salt
1 cup water	1/2 tsp garlic powder
1 (14 1/2oz) can stewed tomatoes	
1/8 tsp pepper	1 1/2cups minute rice
1/2 tsp oregano	

Optional ingredients:
1 small can tomato sauce   1/2 cup additional rice

Brown meat, drain grease. Add corn, water, tomatoes and seasonings. Bring to a boil. Stir in uncooked rice, cover and remove from heat. Let stand for 5 minutes before serving.

Goat Meat Curry

3 lb. goatmeat	2 cardamon
2-3 cloves	3 cinnamon sticks
3-4 bay leaves	1 tsp whole black pepper
1/4 cup oil	4 chopped onions
2 tomatoes (chopped)	2 tbsp tomato puree
1 tbsp garlic paste	1 tbsp ginger paste
1 tbsp red chili powder	1 tbsp coriander powder
1 tsp turmeric powder	1 tbsp garam masala
salt to taste	water for gravy(curry)
2 tbsp fresh coriander leaves (chopped)	

Heat oil in frying pan, add cardamon, cloves, cinnamon sticks, bay leaves, whole black pepper and fry for few seconds. Then add onions and fry until light brown, add ginger garlic paste, tomato, tomato puree, coriander powder, red chili, turmeric and salt to taste. When masala is thoroughly fried and oil comes up add mutton pieces and fry until brown. Then add water cover pan and keep it on low flame until mutton is done. Garnish with chopped coriander (cilantro) leaves and garam masala for a delicious flavor.

72

Hamburger Sausage

Vera Bockelman

It gets hard like summer sausage. Enjoy!

5 pounds hamburger (not ground chuck)

2 1/2tsp salt	**1 tsp liquid smoke**
2 1/2tsp garlic salt	**1/2 tsp dried red pepper**

2 tsp coarsely ground pepper
5 tsp Morton's Tender Quick Salt

Mix all ingredients in a large bowl. Refrigerate for 24 hours. Mix again very well and refrigerate another 24 hours. Shape into rolls. Makes 5 rolls of sausages about 2 inches by 8 inches long. Place on broiler rack pan and bake at 150° F for 8 hours. Turn sausage rolls after 4 hours. Will keep in refrigerator for 5 weeks or freeze.

Easy Beef Stroganoff

Patti Kulick

1 1/2 lb sirloin or round steak	**1 tbsp tomato paste**
1/3 cup sour cream	**2 tbsp butter**
fresh mushrooms (optional)	**1 pound noodles**

salt & pepper to taste
1 medium onion (coarsely chopped)
1 (12 oz) jar Heinz Home-Style Mushroom Gravy

Cut meat into thin strips. In a large skillet, brown meat in 2 tablespoons of butter. Add 1 coarsely chopped onion. Cook until onions are transparent. Stir in Heinz Home-Style Mushroom Gravy (add additional mushrooms if desired – optional). Add tomato paste, salt & pepper to taste. Cover and simmer for 10-20 minutes or until meat is tender. Remove from heat, let stand for 10 minutes. Slowly stir in sour cream. Serve over cooked, buttered noodles.

> It is easier to thinly slice meat if it is partially frozen. This tip will come in very handy when preparing meats for stir fry meals.

73

Favorite Meat Loaf with Sauce   Barbara Linde, Ph.D.

This recipe came from one of my Eastern Star friends in California. My children always complained about my meat loaf until I started using this recipe. It tastes so great!

1 lb ground beef   1 egg (beaten)
1 tbsp brown sugar   dash of salt
1 onion (diced)   dash pepper
1/2 cup cracker crumbs (Ritz crackers)
dash of parsley flakes
1-2 slices of cheese (torn into bits)

Sauce:
3 tbsp brown sugar   1/4 tsp nutmeg
1/4 cup ketchup   1 tsp dry mustard

Combine all meatloaf ingredients together and place in baking pan. Bake at 350° F for 30 minutes, then pour off grease. Mix sauce ingredients together and pour over meat loaf. Cover with foil and bake for 30 minutes or longer, until done.   Makes 1 meatloaf.

Simple Salisbury Steak   Glenna Cruz

1 can cream of mushroom soup   1 egg (beaten)
1/4 cup finely chopped onion   1/3 cup dry bread crumbs
1 1/2 cup sliced mushrooms   1 lb ground beef

In a bowl, mix thoroughly 1/4 cup of soup, beef, bread crumbs, eggs and onion. Shape firmly into 6 patties. In skillet, on medium-high heat, cook patties – a few at a time, until browned on both sides. Drain. Stir in remaining soup and mushrooms. Return patties to skillet. Reduce heat to low – cover. Simmer for 20 minutes or until done, turning patties occasionally. Serves 6.

> Meat loaf will not stick if you place a slice of bacon on the bottom of the pan.

Hamburger Pie

Pamelia Senger

I've been using this recipe since 1972. I got it from a recipe collection I ordered. Serve it with a salad or fresh fruit – DELICIOUS!

1 cup onions (diced)
1 lb hamburger
2 tbsp butter or margarine
1 tsp salt
1/4 tsp pepper
1/2 cup sour cream
paprika to taste
chives or parsley (chopped) to taste

1 tbsp Worcestershire sauce
3 tbsp ketchup or chili sauce
2 tbsp flour
1 9-inch unbaked pie shell
1 cup cottage cheese
2 eggs (slightly beaten)

Cook onions and beef in butter for about 5 minutes, breaking up meat with a fork. Stir in salt, pepper, Worcestershire sauce, ketchup and flour. Turn meat mixture into pie shell. Blend together cottage cheese, sour cream and eggs. Pour over meat mixture. Bake at 350° F for 30–40 minutes. Remove from oven, sprinkle with paprika and either chives or parsley. Makes 6 servings.

Creamed Chicken Over Corn Bread

Patti Kulick

3 chicken breasts
1 stick butter
2 cups chicken broth
1 tsp pimentos (diced)
3/4 cup (small can) evaporated milk
1 can cream of chicken or cream of mushroom soup

1 small onion (chopped)
4 tbsp flour
1 can green peas (drained)
your favorite corn bread

Boil chicken breasts with butter, salt and pepper. Sauté onion in butter until tender. Add flour and stir well. Add soup, milk and broth. Cook until thick. Add cooked chicken, peas and pimentos. Simmer for 30 minutes, stir often. Serve on corn bread.

Chicken Jambalaya

Sharon Foster

We lived in Louisiana for 13 years and went to a small church where we would have a church social once a month. My friend Jone Roe would bring this dish every time and everyone just loved it so I thought that it would be a real good recipe to pass along!

1 stick butter
1 cup white rice
1/2 cup bell pepper (chopped)
1 chicken cooked, (deboned)

1 small can beef broth
2 cans water
1 lb smoked sausage
1 small can onion soup

Boil and debone chicken. Melt butter in a large skillet. Pour in rice and brown over high heat. Add bell pepper and sausage. Add remaining ingredients and put in a large covered casserole dish. Bake at 350° F for 1 hour. Stir once after 30 minutes. Makes 6 servings.

Creole Shrimp

Patsy Williams Hessenflow

1/4 cup butter or margarine
1 large garlic (chopped fine)
1/2 cup celery (chopped)
1 tsp salt
1/4 tsp red pepper
1 lb shrimp (cleaned and cooked)
parsley (a few springs chopped fine)
4 small green onions (chopped fine)
3 1/2 cup tomatoes (no. 2 1/2can)

1 large onion (chopped)
1 cup green pepper (chopped)
2 tbsp flour
1/2 tsp black pepper
1/2 cup water

Melt butter in skillet. Sauté onion, garlic, bell pepper and celery until onion is lightly browned. Blend in flour. Add all remaining ingredients except shrimp. Cover and cook 10 minutes longer. Add shrimp and mix. Serve over hot steamed rice.

Patsy Williams Hessenflow is the granddaughter of Ida and William Treat.

Ma Maw's Brisket
Anne Presley

This was a recipe my mother made many, many times. She was a nurse and worked during the day. She could prepare the roast the night before and cook it after work.

4-6 lb brisket (remove excess fat) 1 tsp salt
1/4 tsp black pepper   1/2 tsp garlic powder
1/2 cup liquid smoke (Colgin brand)

Sauce:
1 cup broth from brisket (remove any fat)
1 can beef broth
1/2 cup liquid smoke   1 cup ketchup
1/4 tsp mustard   4 tbsp brown sugar
1 tsp garlic powder   dash of Tabasco
2 tbsp Worcestershire Sauce (I use Lea & Perrins)

Mix salt, liquid smoke, black pepper and garlic powder together and rub on brisket. Put in a 9x13-inch pan (I use a glass pan). Cover with aluminum foil, refrigerate and marinate overnight. Bake, covered, at 350° F for 2-4 hours. Check for tenderness. Mix all sauce ingredients together in a sauce pan, add ½ can water to rinse out the broth can and bring the mixture to a boil. Pour off excess juices from the brisket pan. Pour sauce over the brisket. Cover with aluminum foil and cook for an additional 45 minutes.

Deer Casserole
John Sowells

1/2 lb deer meat pieces
1 can cream of mushroom soup
1 can cream of celery soup
1 onion (diced)
1 can mushrooms (undrained)
6 potatoes (pared and sliced)
your favorite seasonings

In a large bowl, mix all ingredients together. Pour into a 2-quart casserole dish and bake at 350° F for 1 hour.

Chicken Spaghetti

Vickie Crisenbery

Fix some good garlic bread to go with it!!!

6 chicken tenders	4 oz spaghetti (uncooked)
1 can Rotel tomatoes	Velveeta cheese to taste
1 small can cream of chicken soup	
1 small can cream of mushroom soup	

Boil chicken tenders until done and remove from pot. Add your spaghetti to the boiling water and cook until tender. While spaghetti is boiling, dice your chicken into cubes. Once spaghetti is finished, drain the water and then add your soups, Rotel and chicken. Stir until mixed. Add as much Velveeta cheese as you would like, just depends on how cheesy you want it.

Bird on Nest in Crock

Ray Xiques

This is a "fix it and forget it" dish!

1 1/2 can chicken broth	chicken tenders
3 bay leaves	seasoned salt
dried onion pieces	1 (8 oz) cheddar cheese block
2 tbsp all-purpose flour	1 tsp corn starch
2 chop sticks	
1 1/2 bags frozen mixed vegetables (1 pound bags)	

In a crock pot, place vegetables in the bottom. Add chicken on top of the vegetables. Only 1 layer of chicken – don't overlap. Add broth to just mid-level of chicken, don't cover (you don't want boiled chicken). Distribute bay leaves into the liquid. Sprinkle a bunch of seasoned salt, then dried onion pieces. Cook on high heat for 3 hours. Open pot, make a little hole in the mixture, add flour a little at a time while mixing with chop sticks, then add corn starch, also a little at a time and mix thoroughly. Make a sort of gravy, mix it around the perimeter of the pot with the chop sticks. Remove bay leaves. Slice cheese on top then serve immediately. Enjoy!

Hamburger Corn Bake
Mary Jane Erwin

This is a family favorite recipe.

1 1/2 lb hamburger
salt & pepper to taste
1 cup onion (chopped)
1 cup sour cream
3 cups noodles (cooked and drained)
parmesan cheese to taste
1 can cream of mushroom soup
1 (12 oz) can whole kernel corn (drained)

In a large skillet brown hamburger and onion. Drain corn. Stir corn, cream of mushroom soup, sour cream, salt and pepper together and mix well. Stir in cooked noodles. Place everything in a 2 1/2 quart casserole. Sprinkle parmesan cheese on top. Bake at 350° F for 45 minutes. Serves 8-10.

Bacon-Wrapped Grilled Chicken
Carla Chamberlain

You will need a good spice cabinet for this recipe! It is delicious!!

8 chicken thighs (thoroughly washed and patted dry)
16 slices bacon
Worcestershire Sauce
1/4 cup barbecue sauce
Wickers Marinade

Spices: 1/4 tsp of each:
curry powder
cayenne powder
parsley flakes
tarragon flakes
paprika
blackened seasoning
Tony Checheres Seasoning
garlic powder

Mix all spices together in a small bowl. Rub by pinchfulls all around each chicken thigh until all are coated with spice mixture. Carefully wrap 2 pieces of bacon side-by-side around each thigh and fasten with tooth picks. Place each in a large bowl. When finished, pour barbecue sauce and enough Worcestershire sauce and Wickers Marinade to cover chicken. Allow chicken to marinate for a minimum of 1 hour or overnight. Place on a preheated grill and cook until done. Makes 4 servings.

Chicken and Stuffing Casserole · Cindy Hegerman

8 pieces of chicken
1/2 cup milk
mozzarella cheese to taste

1 stick butter (melted)
2 cans cream of chicken soup
1 pkg stuffing mix

Lay chicken in bottom of a 9x13-inch pan. Heat 1/2 cup milk with the 2 cans of cream of chicken soup. Pour over chicken. Sprinkle with shredded mozzarella cheese, to taste. Cover with the stuffing mix. Pour melted butter over the top. Bake at 350° F for 1 1/4-1 1/2 hours. Makes 4-8 servings depending on how hungry your family is!

Cashew Chicken · Judi Reynolds

1 cup peas (fresh or frozen)
3/4 cup onions (diced)
3/4 cup red bell pepper (diced)
2 cups chicken breast (cut into 1/2 inch slices)
1 (2 1/2 oz) can whole button mushrooms (reserve the liquid)

3/4 cup celery (diced)
1/2 -1 cup cashews

Marinade for Chicken:
1 tbsp light soy sauce
1 tbsp cornstarch
1/2 tsp salt

1 tbsp sherry
1/2 tsp sugar

Sauce Mixture:
1/2 cups reserved mushroom liquid   4 tbsp oil
1 chunk fresh ginger (the size of a quarter, crushed)

Mix sliced chicken with marinade and let stand for 15 minutes. Prepare sauce mixture. Heat wok, pour in 1 tablespoon oil and heat. Stir fry celery and onions for 1-2 minutes. Season lightly with salt and sugar. Set aside. Add 1 tablespoon oil and stir fry the chicken until done. Stir the prepared sauce mixture and pour over chicken, stirring until sauce thickens. Add vegetables, then add cashews. Mix well and serve.

Mexican Casserole

O'Beta Treat Huddleston

1 lb ground beef	1/3 cup onion (chopped)
1 medium garlic (minced)	1 tsp oregano
1 1/2 tsp salt	1/3 cup water
2 cup wide noodles (cooked)	1 cup shredded cheese

Brown (sauté) the beef and onions. Stir to break up beef into small pieces. Combine all ingredients except cheese into an oven safe dish. Bake at 350° F for 30 minutes. Add the cheese in the last few minutes of cooking to melt.

O'Beta Treat Huddleston is the daughter of Ida And William Treat.

Escalloped Potatoes and Frankfurters

Mary Henry Craig

This is a great recipe when you use red potatoes!

2 1/2 lb potatoes (4 large)	2 tbsp butter
2 1/2 tsp prepared mustard	1/2 lb frankfurters
1 cup celery (diced)	1/2 tsp salt
2 cups milk	

Pare and slice potatoes. Cut frankfurters in ½-inch slices. Arrange alternate layers of potatoes, frankfurters and celery in a buttered baking dish. Melt butter in a saucepan and blend in flour, salt, mustard and milk. Stir over direct heat until sauce boils. Pour over ingredients in casserole dish. Bake covered in a 350° F degree oven for 45 minutes to 1 hour. Makes 5 servings.

Mary is the great great granddaughter of W.B. Flippin, great granddaughter of Jim Flippin and granddaughter of Flora Flippin Henry.

Garden Pasta

Sean T. Reynolds

Enjoy! This is a customer favorite in my restaurant.

3 cups fettuccini (cooked)	**2 tbsp butter**
2-3 sprigs fresh thyme	**1/4 cup heavy cream**
1/2 cup zucchini	**1/2 cup yellow squash**
1/2 cup grape tomatoes	**2 tbsp smoked paprika oil**

Italian parsley leaves for garnish
1/4 cup parmesan cheese (freshly grated)
kosher salt and fresh cracked pepper to taste

Cook pasta in boiling salted water according to directions on box. Meanwhile, cut zucchini and yellow squash in half lengthwise. Then slice into 1/4 inch thick slices. Cut tomatoes in half.

In a medium sauce pan (over medium heat) add half the butter and oil, and saute vegetables until tender. Add thyme leaves at the point that the vegetables are almost cooked. Add in cream and cook until reduced by half. Add the rest of the butter, oil, and half of the parmesan cheese. Drain pasta, add to sauce mixture and stir pasta into sauce using tongs. Add additional parmesan cheese on plated pasta and top with a nice green Italian parsley sprig. In addition, this may be served with a nice crusty garlic bread and/or an organic spring mixed salad. Serves 4.

Chef Sean Reynolds is the 2004 and 2005 gold medal recipient in Skills USA Culinary Arts for the State of Arkansas. Together with Master Chef Heiko from Germany, Chef Reynolds cooked for presidents and dignitaries for the opening of the Clinton Presidential Library in Little Rock, Arkansas. Chef Sean has cooked at the world famous Caribou Club in Aspen, Colorado for international dignitaries and Hollywood celebrities. Known for his signature dishes, Sean's dessert dishes are truly "edible art." Sean Reynolds is the owner of Sean's Restaurant & Catering located in Mountain Home, Arkansas.

Chicken Tetrazzini

Flossie Boles

I recently enjoyed this dish in the home of a friend since college and World War II days. Our husbands were stationed at the University of Illinois in Champaign – Urbana. The recipe was probably originally from a cookbook or magazine. And "oldie but goodie."

1 large onion
1/2 cup Velveeta cheese (grated)
1/2 stick butter
2 small cans chopped pimento
1 can chicken broth
3 cups cooked chicken (diced)
1 dash Worcestershire sauce (I use Heinz)
2 small cans of mushrooms
1 can cream of mushroom soup
1 (8 oz) pkg medium wide egg noodles (cooked)
salt & pepper to taste

Chop onion and sauté with butter or margarine. Combine all other ingredients except the cheese. Mix well and pour into a casserole or baking dish. Sprinkle the top with cheese and bake in a preheated 300° F degree oven for 30 minutes. Makes 6-8 servings.

One way to preserve the flavor of fresh herbs is to make herb butter. Let the butter soften, then add finely chopped herbs in any combination, about 2 to 4 tablespoons per stick of butter. The butter freezes well, and you can serve it spread on French bread or with seafood or chicken.

Mexican Casserole

Teresa Robideau

This is a composite of 2 different recipes from Air Force friends.

1 lb ground beef
onion to taste
garlic to taste
1 can cream of celery soup
1 can enchilada sauce
1 small can green chilies (chopped)

sour cream (optional)
1/3 cup mild salsa
1 lg bag tortilla chips
1 pkg grated mexican cheese

Brown beef, onion and garlic. Drain off excess fat. Add soup, enchilada sauce, chilies and salsa. Cook to blend flavors and ingredients. Crush tortilla chips. Using an 11x7x2-inch casserole dish, start layering ingredients; crushed chips, meat sauce & cheese. Continue layering until mixtures are all used up. Bake at 350° F for 30 minutes. Serves 6-8.

Note: The recipe freezes well in individual servings and can be reheated in a microwave. Deer hamburger is also tasty when used in place of ground beef.

Sunday Dinner Pot Roast

Arne Knapp

This pot roast always comes out fork tender!

3 lb beef roast
3 stalks celery (diced)
1 bag frozen pearl onions
8 small red potatoes (optional)
1 (2 lb) bag carrots (peeled, ready-to-eat)
2 cans cream of chicken soup (undiluted)

Cut roast into 2 pieces. Brown roasts on both sides in small roaster or roasting pan. Remove soup from cans and mix together in a bowl. Pour soup over meat. Bake, covered, at 350° F for 1 1/2 hours.   Add carrots, onions, potatoes and celery and stir into soup. Bake, covered, for 1 hour longer, until meat is tender and vegetables are done.

Substitution: Use pork roast instead of beef roast. Use cream of mushroom soup instead of cream of chicken soup.

If you like ribs like I do and don't want to pay high restuarant prices, you can easily make these ribs yourself. The slow cooking process is the secret to the tenderness of the ribs. I think you will find that these ribs will be some of the best you have ever tasted!

Barbecue Sauce:

1 cup ketchup	1 cup vinegar
1/2 cup dark corn syrup	2 tsp sugar
1/2 tsp salt	1/4 tsp garlic powder
1/4 tsp onion powder	1/4 tsp Tobasco

Combine all ingredients in a sauce pan over high heat and bring to a boil. Reduce heat and simmer 30-45 minutes until sauce thickens. If sauce is too thick, thin with more vinegar.

4 lb baby back pork ribs or spare ribs

Divide ribs into 3 or 4 rib serving size portions. Tear aluminum foil into pieces about 6 inches longer than the rib sections. Coat the ribs front and back with the BBQ sauce. Put rib section on a piece of foil and wrap tightly. Place wrapped ribs in a baking dish, seam side up. Bake at 300° F for 2-2 1/2hours, until meat shrinks back from the cut end of the bone. Remove cooked ribs from foil and coat with BBQ sauce again. Grill ribs on a hot charcoal grill for 2-4 minutes on each side, until BBQ sauce is lightly charred. Serve with BBQ sauce.

> Tenderize pot roast or stewing meat by using two cups of hot tea as a cooking liquid.

Ham Loaf

1 large can of pears (drain and reserve syrup)

Ham loaf:

1 1/2 pounds ham (ground)	1 lb fresh pork (ground)
1 cup bread crumbs	1 cup milk
2 eggs (beaten)	2 tbsp vinegar
2 tsp dry mustard	

Sauce:

1 cup pear syrup	1 cup brown sugar
1/2 tsp cloves	1/2 tsp allspice

2 tbsp prepared mustard
1 (12oz) jar of marmalade (I use 3/4 of a jar)

Mix meat ingredients, shape into loaf and place in large baking dish. Bake at 350° F for 1 hour. Remove from oven. Drain pears and reserve syrup. Place pears in dish around ham loaf. Bring sauce ingredients to a boil, cook for 5 minutes. Return ham loaf to oven and baste with sauce while cooking for 30 minutes more. Thicken remaining sauce with 1 tablespoon cornstarch dissolved in 1 tablespoon water. Serve over ham loaf.

Herb Tips

* To preserve summer herbs for winter soups and stews, make herb cubes in the freezer. Chop up your herbs and place them in ice cube trays, then cover with water and freeze.
* To preserve the color and flavor, use boiling water to fill the tray (this blanches the herbs).
* Some herbs, like cilantro, keep better when frozen in oil. Mince the herb in a food processor, then introduce olive oil until you produce a fine puree. Pour into ice cube trays or bags and freeze.
* When introducing the frozen herbs to recipes, remember that they contain water or oil. If this will throw off the recipe's consistency, thaw and drain the cubes first.

Lasagna

Patti Boonstra

Do you like to entertain buffet style? Lasagna makes a perfect main dish. Partner it with a crisp salad for a delicious meal!

1 lb ground beef	1/3 lb ground lean pork
3/4 cup chopped onion	1 clove garlic (minced)
1 (1 lb) can tomatoes	1 (15 oz) can tomato sauce
2 tbsp sugar	2 1/2 tsp salt, divided
1 tsp basil leaves	3 tbsp parsley flakes, divided
1 tsp oregano leaves	

3/4 lb mozzarella cheese, shredded
1 cup parmesan cheese, divided (grated)
2 (12 oz cartons) creamed cottage cheese (3 cups total)
1 (8 oz) pkg lasagna noodles (cooked and well drained)

Stir and cook ground beef, pork, onion and garlic in a large saucepan until meat is brown and onion is tender. Drain off all fat. Add tomatoes and break up with a fork. Stir in tomato sauce, 2 tablespoons parsley flakes, sugar, 1 teaspoon salt and basil. Heat to boiling, stirring occasionally. Reduce heat; simmer uncovered for 1 hour or until mixture is the consistency of spaghetti sauce. Mix cottage cheese, 1/2 cup Parmesan cheese, 1 tablespoon parsley flakes, 1 1/2 tsp salt and oregano. Reserve ½ cup meat sauce for a thin top layer. In an ungreased baking pan, 9x13-inches, layer 1/4 each of the noodles, remaining meat sauce, the mozzarella cheese and cottage cheese mixture. Repeat 3 times. Spread reserved meat sauce over the top; sprinkle with 1/2 cup Parmesan cheese. Bake uncovered at 350° F for 45 minutes. Serves 12.

Tip: If lasagna is refrigerated before baking, cook an additional 15 minutes. Let stand 15 minutes before cutting.

Pilgrim Stew – New Mexico Style   Billie Thomas Daniel

This became a family favorite while living in New Mexico where we first learned about green chilies and the many ways to use it. Getting the venison was a fun time. We used it as a family-get-away down in the Guadalupe Mountains, camping by ourselves or with other families! Lot of fond memories!

3 lb venison (cubed)	1 cup onion (chopped)
1 cup Bisquick	2 tbsp bell pepper flakes
1 tsp salt	4 carrots (sliced)
1/2 tsp pepper	4–5 potatoes (cubed 1 1/2 inch)
1/2 tsp paprika	1 tsp seasoning blend
4 tbsp shortening or oil	2 beef bouillon cubes
3 cups water	

1/4 -1/2 cup chopped green chilies topped with garlic powder

Trim all the fat and gristle from the venison. Mix Bisquick, salt pepper and paprika in a plastic bag. Add meat and shake to coat. Brown meat in melted shortening. Add onion and sauté until limp but not browned. Place potatoes and carrots in the bottom of a 3 1/2 quart or larger crock pot. Add meat and onions. Add the remaining ingredients except for the chilies. Add seasoning blend and bouillon cubes. Add 3 cups of water, set crock pot on low and cook for 24 hours. Check and add additional water if needed. An hour before serving, add green chilies. Continue cooking on low until meat is tender. Makes approximately 12 servings.

DESSERTS

Building the Bull Shoals Dam

Between 1915-1927 there were several major destructive floods in the White River Basin. The spring flood of 1927 covered four million acres of prime farmland. For flood control, construction of the Bull Shoals dam began in June, 1947, and was completed in July, 1952.

After World War II ended many of the men from Marion County returned home only to find there were no jobs. The building of Bull Shoals Dam was a lifesaver for the economy of Marion County. People came in droves hoping to find work. They slept wherever they could pitch a tent, rent a spot in a bar, or simply slept in backyards.

The building materials for the dam were transported by two specially constructed projects. A conveyor belt 30 inches wide and 7.8 miles long carried the rock aggregate from Lee's Mountain near Flippin to the dam site concrete plant. The belt ran three shifts, 24 hours a day, for approximately six years. A railroad spur was built to move the steel, cement and heavy equipment from the Cotter railhead.

Heavy blasting at the quarry caused damage to many residences, practically every business in Flippin, as well as the area near the rock quarry located on the Wilson farm on Lee's Mountain. To meet demand, new businesses sprang up in Flippin and prospered. The need for new homes and additional housing became apparent and construction of these followed in Flippin and the surrounding areas. A new paved highway from Flippin to the dam site was constructed.

The Bull Shoals hydro-electric dam is the fifth largest concrete dam in the United States.

Dorothy Rose

A Slice of Flippin History

Dorothy was born in Bruno Arkansas on December 2, 1909 and moved to Flippin when she married her husband Ran on December 24, 1929. Together they had 3 children, Bill, Syble and Madeline, nic-named Snooks.

Dorothy's life in the Ozarks reads like a history of the community. She was a cook on a wood stove with no electricity at the Rose Restaurant and Hotel (see photo of the Rose Hotel on page 6). Dorothy worked 7 days a week from sunrise until well after dark to help provide for her growing family.

Over the years, Dorothy left the Rose Hotel and worked for other restaurants in the area, including Gaston's White River Resort where, in addition to her normal duties, she also baked her famous "Abe Lincoln Pie" to the delight of customers.

Never afraid of hard work, in 1960, Dorothy helped her children start a new restaurant known as "Mr. Bass" in Bull Shoals where Dorothy helped the kids with the cooking and together they created a very popular, busy business. The original name of the restaurant came from the family's nic-name for son Bill!

When asked what were the most significant changes Dorothy

Dorothy Rose

90

witnessed in the community over the years, she said, "The drunks are not on the streets of Flippin today as they were in the 30's when the streets were dirt and I started working in the restaurants." In addition to working very hard for her entire life, Dorothy also enjoys quilting and has created many beautiful quilts. She is also proud of the fact that she has 5 grand children, 10 great grandchildren and 5 great great grandchildren!

Below is a copy of Dorothy's very famous, very popular Abe Lincoln Pie which was featured in many local restaurants over the years. In fact, most people know Dorothy as the Abe Lincoln Pie woman!

Abe Lincoln Pie   Dorothy Rose

1 1/2 cups sugar	1 sq bitter sweet chocolate (grated)
1 1/2 cups milk	1 tsp vanilla extract
4 eggs	Dash of Salt
1 1/2 pkg Knox gelatin	3 (1/2 pint) cartons whipping cream
1/4 cup warm water	1 graham cracker pie crust

Mix sugar, salt and milk. Add egg yolks. Cook over low heat until it boils, stirring constantly. Remove from heat. Add vanilla and gelatin mix (mix gelatin in 1/4 cup warm water before adding to mixture). Set aside to cool. Beat egg whites until stiff. Beat whipping cream. Use hand mixer to fold whipped cream and beaten egg white together. Add sauce slowly to whipped cream and egg white mixture. Pour immediately into a graham cracker crust. Top with grated chocolate. Chill pie in refrigerator 3 to 4 hours.

Grannie Treat's Applesauce Cookies

Nadyne Wood Aikman

This was my favorite cookie made by Grannie. She gave me this recipe when I married. (Grannie is Ida Speer Treat).

3/4 cup shortening
1 egg
2 1/4 cup flour
1/2 tsp baking soda
3/4 tsp cinnamon
1 cup raisins

1 cup brown sugar
1/2 cup applesauce
1/2 cup nuts (chopped)
1/2 tsp salt
1/4 cup cloves

Cream together shortening and egg; add sugar to creamed mixture. Sift dry ingredients. Alternate dry ingredients with applesauce into mixture. Blend well. Add nuts and chill dough for 30 minutes. Bake at 350° F for 8 –12 minutes.

Nadyne is the granddaughter of Ida and William Treat.

Gram's Ginger Creams

Pearl Butcher Baker

This recipe was handed down from my grandmother who was born in Vinton, Iowa around 1870. She and Grandfather had 12 children, 1 of which was my dad, born in 1895 on their homestead in eastern Montana along the Little Missouri River. Everyone knew her as "Gram" and she was loved by all children and anyone who met her.

1/2 cup shortening
1 cup strong coffee
1 cup brown sugar
1 cup molasses
1 egg (beaten slightly)

1 tsp baking soda
1 tsp ginger
1 tsp cinnamon
1/2 tsp salt
4 cups flour (sifted)

Cream together wet ingredients using mixer. Sift together dry ingredients and combine with wet, mixing until smooth. Press onto a large cookie sheet and bake at 400° F on the middle rack for approximately 30 minutes or until toothpick inserted into center comes out clean. Use a cream cheese or vanilla frosting on top, cut into squares and serve warm. Makes approximately 20 squares.

Nieman Marcus Brownies
Sheila Middleton

1 box Butter Pecan cake mix	1 stick melted margarine
1 egg	

Topping:

1 lb box powdered sugar	1 stick melted margarine
2 eggs	1 cup pecans (chopped)
1 pkg cream cheese (softened)	

Mix the cake mix, egg and melted margarine together. Press into an 11x17-inch pan. Mix together well the powdered sugar, melted margarine, cream cheese, 2 eggs and pecans. Spread over cake mixture. Bake at 300° F for approximately 55 minutes or until done.

Butterscotch Bars
Linda (Williams) Lane

1 1/2 cups flour	1/2 cup corn syrup
1/2 tsp salt	3/4 cup brown sugar
1 pkg butterscotch chips	1 (12 oz) can mixed nuts
2 tbsp + 1/2 cup butter (softened)	

Mix flour, salt, brown sugar and butter together. Press into a 9x13-inch pan (sprayed with Pam or another nonstick spray). Bake at 350° F for 10 minutes. Remove from the oven. Spread nuts over mixture. Mix together butterscotch chips, syrup and butter. Melt mixture over low heat. Pour over crust and nuts. Return to oven at 350° F for 10 minutes. Let cool. Cut into bars.

Poor Man's Cake
Inis Mae Proctor

1 1/2 cups flour (all purpose)	1 cup sugar
3 tbsp cocoa	6 tbsp butter
1 tbsp baking soda	1/2 tsp salt
1 cup water	1 tbsp vinegar
1 tsp vanilla extract	

Mix all ingredients together and pour into an 8x8-inch square pan. Bake at 350° F for 20 – 25 minutes.

Vinegar Cobbler

Russelline Wood Smith

2 1/2 cups sugar	1/4 tsp salt
1/4 cup cornstarch	2 1/2 cup water
1/2 tsp cinnamon	2 pie crusts (cooked)
3/4 cup vinegar	
1 tbsp butter	

Mix sugar, cornstarch, cinnamon and salt together well in a large heavy saucepan. Add vinegar and mix well. Add water, mix well and bring mixture to a boil. Continue to boil until mixture becomes transparent. Add butter and cool to lukewarm. Pour vinegar mixture onto cooked pie crusts and serve warm. Makes 2 pies.

Russelline Wood Smith is the granddaughter of Ida And William Treat.

Hello Dollies

Glenn Chamberlain D.D.S.

For special tastes, chip types and nut type can be changed.

1 1/3 pkg graham crackers	5 1/2 oz chocolate chips
1 (14 oz) can condensed milk	5 1/2oz butterscotch chips
1 (6 oz) bag Baker's angel flake coconut	
1/4 lb margarine, or butter (1 stick)	
2/3 to 1 cup pecan pieces (break up whole pecans)	

Melt 1 stick margarine (or butter) and pour into a 9x13-inch glass pan, swirl onto sides 2/3 depth of pan (pan is usually 1 1/2 to 2 inches deep). Grate graham crackers in blender and pour into pan over butter. Smooth out evenly over bottom of pan only. (This can be done with a large spoon). Next place coconut evenly in pan – DO NOT compact or press coconut into the pan. Now pour sweetened condensed milk evenly over all of the coconut; then sprinkle both types of chips over milk and finally scatter pecans evenly over the top. Bake at 350° F until bubbling can be seen throughout the middle of the dish (usually 30 to 35 minutes). Do not overcook. You are NOT looking for browning during cooking. Remove from oven after bubbling in center of pan occurs. Let cool, cut and enjoy!

Cake in a Jar
Betty Wood

This recipe is easy and fun to bring out when family and friends come over. I made this recipe for Christmas gifts and it was a big hit!

3 eggs
2 cups sugar
1 cup vegetable oil
1 tsp vanilla extract
2 cups all-purpose-flour
4 cups apples (chopped and peeled)

2 tsp ground cinnamon
1 tsp baking soda
1/2 tsp salt
3/4 cup pecans (chopped)

Mix eggs, sugar, vegetable oil and vanilla. Mix well. Mix together flour, cinnamon, soda and salt. Add and mix well. Stir in apples and nuts. Pour into a well-greased, pint sized jar (wide mouth with no necks), filling only half full. Wipe jar rims just like you are canning. Bake at 350° F for 30–40 minutes. Baking times may vary depending on your oven so keep a check on them after 30 minutes. Remove 1 jar at a time from the oven. Wipe sealing edge again. Put on lid, ring and screw tight. Jar will seal as it cools. Store as you would regular canned goods.

Old Fashioned Blueberry Cupcakes
Melody Dennis

My grandmother baked these cupcakes for my mother and my mother baked them for me. These cupcakes are very tasty and moist.

2 1/4 cups flour
3 tsp baking powder
1/2 tsp salt
1 1/2 cups sugar
1 cup milk

1/4 cup extra flour for dusting berries
2 eggs
1 tsp vanilla extract
1 1/2 cups blueberries
1/2 cup Crisco shortening

Sift dry ingredients into mixing bowl. Add Crisco and 3/4 cups milk. Mix well then add 1/4 cup milk. Mix together eggs and vanilla. Combine and blend for 2 minutes at medium speed, then 1 additional minute at low speed. Flour blueberries with 1/4 cup flour. Shake off excess flour. Fold blueberries into mixture. Fill baking cups 3/4 full then sprinkle sugar on top. Bake at 375° F for 25 minutes or until brown. Makes 18 cupcakes.

Pound Cake

Nadyne Wood Aikman/Russelline Wood Smith

1 lb butter or oleo	1 lb powdered sugar
6 eggs, divided	3 cups sifted flour
2 tsp vanilla extract	1 tsp vanilla butter nut flavoring

Beat butter until light and fluffy; add powdered sugar alternately with 2 of the eggs. Beat well. Then add flour mixed with salt and alternate with remaining 4 eggs. Beat well after each addition. Add flavorings. Beat again. The more you beat, the lighter the texture of your cake will be. Bake in a bundt pan or an angel food cake pan at 325° F for 1 hour. Watch closely as it browns quickly.

Nadyne Wood Aikman and Russelline Wood Smith are the granddaughters of Ida and William Treat.

Mom's Coffee Cake

Sheila (Osborn) Luck

I'm not sure how Mom got this recipe but I always remember her making it for Daddy. Each time I make this I feel like I'm home again. I will always know Flippin, Arkansas as my home.

1 cup raisins	2/3 cup coffee
1/2 tsp cinnamon	1/3 cup butter
1/3 cup oil	1 cup sugar
2 eggs	1 1/2 cups all-purpose
1/2 tsp baking powder	1/2 tsp baking soda

Glaze:
1 1/2 cups powdered sugar   1/4 cups coffee

Place raisins and cinnamon in bowl and pour coffee over to soak. In another bowl, mix together remaining ingredients until smooth and creamy. Add raisin mixture. Pour onto a small ungreased cookie sheet and bake at 350° F for 20 minutes. Mix glaze and top cake after it has fully cooled.

Sheila (Osborn) Luck is the daughter of Lloyd & Anita Osborn.

Aunt Ruth's Chocolate Cake

Mildred Stewart

This recipe was given to me by my sister-in-law Ruth Stewart. It is undoubtedly the best chocolate cake I have ever eaten. My family always refers to this cake as "Aunt Ruth's Chocolate Cake." Ruth passed away recently and I think she would be honored to have her recipe in this cookbook.

2 cups flour	2 eggs
4 tbsp cocoa	1/2 cup buttermilk
1/2 tsp salt	2 cups sugar
1 tsp baking soda	1/2 cup Crisco shortening
1 cup boiling water	

Combine flour, cocoa and salt together – set aside. Cream sugar and Crisco. Add eggs and mix well. To this mixture add flour mixture, alternating with buttermilk. Batter will be very stiff. Boil water. Add baking soda to boiling water, stir well until dissolved and pour into cake mixture. Mix well and quickly pour into cake pans. Bake at 325° F oven for 40 minutes. Makes 1-2-layer cake or 1- 9x13-inch loaf cake. Frost with a favorite powdered sugar or store bought frosting.

Butterfinger Cake

Amanda Alexander

butter cake mix	king size Butterfinger candy bar
creamy cool whip	caramel ice cream topping

Bake cake mix like normal. Let cake cool. Squeeze caramel on top of cake, smash Butterfinger bar up and sprinkle on top of the caramel. Spread Cool Whip on top. Refrigerate and serve!

Depression Apple Spice Cake

Dorothy Cotch

This is an heirloom recipe – a favorite of those who like a heavy, moist & spicy cake.

2 cups sugar
1/2 cup shortening
1 apple (peeled and grated)
1 tsp baking soda
1 tsp cinnamon
1 tsp ground cloves
1 cup nuts (chopped, optional)

2 cups strong coffee
2 cups raisins
2 cups flour
2 tsp baking powder
1 tsp allspice
1 tsp nutmeg

Simmer sugar, coffee, shortening, raisins and apple for 10 minutes, stirring occasionally. Cool 10 minutes. Blend together the flour, baking soda, baking powder, cinnamon, allspice, cloves and nutmeg and stir into saucepan mixture. Mix in nuts. Pour batter into well-greased and floured 13x9-inch pan. Bake at 350° F for 25-30 minutes, or until toothpick inserted in center comes out clean. Cool. Dust with powdered sugar, cut and serve.

Pumpkin Cake

Bonnie Smith

I have had this recipe for about 20 years and it is a family favorite especially at Thanksgiving. Since it is so easy to do, I take it to a lot of potlucks!

3 eggs
1 yellow cake mix
1 cup butter (melted)
1 lg can Libby pumpkin pie filling
1 (12oz) can evaporated milk

1 1/2 cups sugar
1 cup pecans (chopped)

Combine pumpkin, evaporated milk, eggs and sugar. Pour into 9x13-inch pan. Sprinkle with dry cake mix. Pat down into pumpkin mixture. Sprinkle with pecans. Drizzle over all with melted butter. Bake at 350° F for 50 minutes. Serve with cool whip. Enjoy!

Fig Cake

This is an old family recipe from my grandmother, Fannie Kate Allen Meador of Alabama and Mississippi, that goes back to the 1890-1900s. I occasionally serve it to our guests at White Hole Resort in Flippin, Arkansas.

2 cups flour (all-purpose)	1 tsp cinnamon
1 tsp ground cloves	1 tsp nutmeg
1 tsp salt	1 tsp baking soda
1 tsp vanilla extract	1 1/2 cups sugar
1 cup buttermilk	1 cup cooking oil
3 eggs	1 cup pecans
1 cup fig preserves (chopped or mashed)	

Sauce:

1 cup sugar	1/2 cup buttermilk
1 tsp vanilla	1 tbsp white corn syrup
1/2 tsp baking soda	1/2 to 1 stick butter
4 tbsp brandy (optional)	

Mix dry ingredients. Mix oil, eggs, milk and vanilla in a blender. Stir into dry ingredients. Add figs and fold in nuts. Bake in tube pan or bundt pan at 350° F for 1 hour or until brown. Stick holes in cake with a fork. To make sauce, mix all ingredients together and boil for 3 minutes, stirring constantly. Pour over warm cake. Serve warm or cool. Delicious served warm with whipped cream. Easily serves 15 to 20 people.

White Hole Resort is located at 4971 MC 7001, Flippin Arkansas 72634. 870-453-2913 telephone. See page 132 for more information.

A cake will keep longer if you place half an apple in the cake tin when storing.

Make a better chocolate cake by adding a teaspoon of vinegar to your cake mix.

Lemon Cheesecake
Kristen Wilkes

1 1/4 cups graham cracker crumbs
1 (8oz) pkg cream cheese
1 stick melted butter
1 cup sugar
1 small pkg lemon gelatin
1 tsp vanilla extract
1 cup boiling water
1 cup evaporated milk (chilled)
3 tbsp lemon juice

Mix graham cracker crumbs and melted butter together. Press into a 9x13-inch dish. Reserve a small portion of crumb mixture for topping. Chill at least 1 hour. Dissolve gelatin in boiling water. Add lemon juice and cool. Cream sugar and cream cheese together and combine with gelatin mixture. Mix in vanilla and stir until smooth (keep cool). Whip chilled evaporated milk until stiff. Fold into gelatin mixture. Pour into graham cracker crust and sprinkle remaining crumbs on top. Chill at least 12 hours before serving.

Strawberry Magic Cake
Mrs. John (Tootsie) Sonntag

This recipe "found" on-line. It is truly different and good!

1 (10 oz) bag mini-marshmallows   1 pkg yellow cake mix
1 pkg small strawberry Jell-O   2/3 cup cold water
1 (16 oz) frozen strawberries (slightly thawed)

Spread marshmallows evenly over bottom of a 9x13-inch pan prepared with "Pam" or other pan coating. Prepare cake batter according to package instructions and spread evenly over marshmallows. Sprinkle dry Jell-O powder evenly over cake batter. Spoon slightly thawed strawberries here and there over the gelatin powder. Drizzle the 2/3 cup water evenly over all. Do not stir! Slip cake carefully onto center rack of a 350° F oven. Bake for 55 minutes to1 hour, until skewer inserted into center of cake comes out clean and the top is golden brown. Let set on a rack to cool (in pan) at least 30 minutes. Refrigerator leftovers. Serves 8.

Mother's Best Fudge Cake

Karen Rounceville

This was a birthday favorite for my husband. After he passed away – now my daughters and grand children want it for their birthdays too!

Chocolate Mixture:
3 oz unsweetened chocolate
1/2 cup milk

2/3 cup sugar
1 egg (well beaten)

Cake Mixture:
1 tsp vanilla extract
2 cups flour
1 tsp baking soda
1 cup sugar

2 eggs
1/2 cup shortening
2/3 cup milk

Chocolate Mixture: Combine chocolate, 1/2 cups milk, 1 well beaten egg and 2/3 cups sugar in a saucepan. Cook over low heat. Stir constantly until thick. Let cool.

Cake Mixture: Stir shortening to soften. Gradually add 1 cup of sugar and cream the two together. Add vanilla. Add 2 eggs (1 at a time). Add flour, baking soda and salt alternately (this is important) with 2/3 cups milk. Beat after each addition. Blend in chocolate mixture. Pour batter into 2 greased round cake pans. Bake at 350° F for 25–30 minutes. Makes 12 servings.

Apricot Bars

Ruby Williams

This is a treat that won't stay around long!

1/4 cup butter
1 egg
1/2 tsp salt
1 (8 oz) jar apricot preserves
1 1/2 cups coconut (shredded)

1 cup sugar
1 1/2 tsp vanilla extract
2 cups flour
1 cup walnuts (chopped)

Cream butter, sugar, eggs and vanilla together. Mix in flour, coconut and salt and stir well. Reserve 3/4 cup of this for your topping. Spread the remaining mixture into a 9x11-inch pan. Spread apricot preserves over top of mixture in pan. Sprinkle nuts over preserves. Crumble or spoon the remaining 3/4 cups of dough over the top (a little here and there). Bake at 350° F for 30 minutes. Let cool slightly and cut into bars. Makes 24 bars.

Mrs. Field's Cookies

Mike Osmundson

I just love chocolate chip cookies. I don't know if this is the 'real' Mrs. Field's cookie recipe, or not, but these sure are good!

1 cup butter	1 cup sugar
1 cup brown sugar	2 eggs
1 tsp vanilla	2 cups flour
1/2 tsp salt	1 tsp baking powder
1 tsp baking soda	1 (12 oz) bag chocolate chips
1 1/2 cups nuts, any kind	
2 1/2 cups regular oatmeal	

(measure first, then grind to a powder in blender)

Cream together butter, sugar and brown sugar. Add eggs and vanilla. Mix together flour, ground oatmeal, salt, baking powder and soda. Add and mix in. Add chocolate chips and nuts. Make golf ball size cookies spaced 2 inches apart on greased cookie sheet. Bake at 375° F for 6 minutes. Makes 5 dozen cookies.

No Bake Cookies

Margaret (Maggie) Kapelski

I received a cookbook back in 1988 from a lady who is near and dear to my heart. She compiled this small book and gave it to me as a Christmas present. My lady has passed away recently so I cherish my book even more. Her name was Margie Casteel Knight. She and her husband, Lewis, were more than bosses to me. This no-bake recipe takes 10-15 minutes to put together, making it fast and tasty!

2 cups sugar	1/2 cup peanut butter
3 tbsp cocoa	1 tsp vanilla extract
1 stick butter	3 cups quick cook oats
pinch of salt	1/2 cup milk

Boil sugar, cocoa, butter, salt and milk for 2 minutes (do not start timing until mixture starts to boil). Add peanut butter, vanilla and oats. Beat until stiff enough to drop on a cookie sheet or waxed paper. Let cool before serving.

Willy's Prize Peanut Butter Cookies
Ken Wilson

Life is short, so eat dessert first! The ultimate comfort food is a cookie, best hot from the oven with a glass of milk for 'dunking'.

2 1/2 cups flour	1 cup sugar
1 cup brown sugar (packed)	1/2 tsp salt
1 cup (2 sticks) butter	2 eggs
2 tsp vanilla extract	1 tsp baking soda
1/2 cup party peanuts	

1 1/2 cups Jif Crunchy Peanut butter
(I use Jif, there really is a difference in peanut butter!)

Cream the butter and sugars together until smooth. Beat in the eggs and vanilla. Add peanut butter and mix well. Mix dry ingredients together and add to peanut butter mixture, beating until very well mixed adding the peanuts while mixing. Roll into logs about 1 1/2inches in diameter and cut into 1inch lengths. Place on cookie sheet and press the pieces down with a fork to make a criss-cross pattern. Bake at 350° F for 9 minutes. (Ovens vary, so adjust time as necessary). Remove from oven and let cool on sheet for several minutes then place the cookies on a cooling rack.

Note: If you use 2 cookie sheets and bake on an upper and lower rack, switch the sheets at 5 minutes to ensure baking consistency of the cookies.

To soften rock-hard brown sugar, simply add a slice of soft bread to the package and close the bag tightly. In a few hours the sugar will be soft again.

Scottish Oatmeal Trilby's

Linda Armstrong

Oatmeal Trilby's are thought to have originated in Scotland. My Great-great-great grandfather, Dougald Duncan Kennedy, was born in 1828 in Argyleshire county in Scotland and emigrated to America in July, 1851. My great-grandmother passed this recipe to my grandmother, who in turn, passed the recipe to my mother. We often wonder, with our Scottish heritage, if the original recipe did indeed come from Scotland.

1 cups butter	1 1/4 cups flour
1 cup brown sugar (packed)	1 tsp soda
1/4 tsp salt	1/4 cups hot water
2 cups regular oatmeal (not quick oats)	

Date Filling:

1/2 cup water	1/2 cup sugar
1 tbsp lemon juice	1/4 cup chopped nuts
1 1/4 cups (8 oz) dates, or part raisins	

Sift, then measure flour. Sift again with soda and salt. Cream butter and sugars slowly. Add the dry ingredients, alternately with the hot water. Add the oatmeal. Form into rolls, wrap in plastic and chill overnight, or for several hours. Cut in 1/4 inch slices and bake on greased cookie sheet at 350° F for approximately 10 minutes. After removing from oven, let cookies stand for a few minutes before removing from cookie sheet. To make date filling: cook the chopped dates, water and sugar slowly, until the dates are soft. Remove from heat and beat until smooth. Add lemon juice and nuts, mix well and let cool. Spread date filling on a cookie and top with another cookie to make a sandwich.

Optional: To make date filled cookies in 1 step, place a cut cookie on cookie sheet. Place 1 tbsp of date filling in center of cookie. Place another cookie over the top of the filling with a slit cut in center, or design cut out with 1/2 inch cookie cutter. Press edges of cookie together.

Pumpkin Chocolate Chip Cookies

Jeanell Vigna

2 1/4 cups flour
1 tsp baking powder
1/2 tsp salt
1 cup sugar
2 large eggs
1 1/2 tsp pumpkin pie spice
1/2 tsp baking soda
1 cup butter (2 sticks)
1 (15 oz) can cooked pumpkin
1 tsp vanilla extract
1 (12 oz) bag semi-sweet chocolate morsel (2 cups)

Glaze:
1 cup powdered sugar
1/2 tsp vanilla extract
1/2 -1 tbsp milk

Combine flour, pumpkin pie spice, baking powder, baking soda and salt. In another bowl, beat butter and sugar until creamy. Beat in pumpkin, eggs, vanilla. To this mixture, slowly combine flour mixture. Fold in chocolate morsels. Drop by tablespoons onto greased cookie sheets. Bake at 375° F for 15-20 minutes until edges are lightly browned. Cool on baking sheets for 2 minutes before removing. Mix glaze and frost cookies.

Pinto Bean Pie

Lily Bell Hurst

1/2 cup cooked pinto beans (mashed)
2 eggs
1 tsp vanilla extract
1 stick oleo
1 cup coconut
1 1/2 cup sugar

Mix all ingredients together until well blended throughout. Pour into an unbaked pie shell. Bake at 350° F for 30 minutes.

Lily Bell Hurst was born in Marion County in Flippin, Arkansas. Lily is affectionately known as "Aunt Bell" to all her family and friends. She grew up on a farm with her typical, hard-working family during a time when there weren't any of the technological luxuries we enjoy today. She is a woman of great morality and high Christian standards.

Impossible Pumpkin Pie
Inis Mae Proctor

1 can pumpkin
1 can milk
1/2 cup self rising flour
1 tsp vanilla extract

1/4 cup brown sugar
2 eggs
spices (nutmeg & cinnamon)
3/4 cup sugar

Put all ingredients in a blender and beat for 1 minute. Pour into an 8-inch pie plate and cook at 350° F until thick (approximately 30 minutes). When cool, cover with Cool Whip.

Out of This World Pie
Mikki Washam

1 cup coconut
1 cup chopped pecans
1/4 cup lemon juice
1 large carton Cool Whip
1 can Eagle Brand sweetened condensed milk
1 large can crushed pineapple (drained)
2 graham cracker pie crusts

Mix ingredients together, pour into pie shell and chill. Be sure to top with Cool Whip before serving. Makes 2 pies.

Million Dollar Pie
In Memory of Jeanette Flippin

Jeanette spent her lifetime cooking in restaurants in Marion and Baxter Counties. She would get to work very early in the morning so she could get the pies baked. She certainly made delicious pies!

1 cup nuts (chopped)
2 baked pie shells
1/2 cup lemon juice
1 large can crushed pineapple (drained)
1 (12 oz) carton frozen Cool Whip
1 can eagle brand sweetened condensed milk
maraschino cherries for garnish

Beat milk. Add lemon juice, pineapple, nuts and cool whip. Pour into 2 baked pie shells. Add maraschino cherries for garnish.

French Raisin Pie

Fern Benton

1/2 cup butter (softened)
1 1/2 cups sugar
3 eggs
1 cup raisins
1 cup pecans (chopped)

1/2 tsp cinnamon
1/2 tsp allspice
2 tbsp vinegar
1 9-inch unbaked pie shell

Cream softened butter and add sugar slowly while beating. Add eggs, 1 at a time and beat until blended. Add raisins and nuts. Mix and stir in spices and vinegar. Pour into a 9-inch pie shell and bake at 350° F for 35 to 40 minutes.

Quick Coconut Pie

Althea Hudson

1 1/2 cups sugar
1/2 cup flour
2 tsp vanilla extract

2 cups coconut
4 eggs
1 stick butter (softened)

Mix all ingredients together and pour into a buttered pie pan. Bake at 350° F for 45 minutes.

Pie Crust

Gail Flippin

This recipe was given to me as a young girl by an aunt of mine, while growing up in Kansas. I have used it for about 35 years and it has never failed.

1/4 tsp salt
1 egg
2 cups flour (all purpose, sifted)

1 cup Crisco shortening
1 tsp vinegar

Mix ingredients with fork or pastry cutter until crumbly. Add enough water to make a sticky dough. Roll out on floured surface to size of an 8 or 9-inch pie pan. Makes crust for 1 pie.

Oatmeal Crunch Pear Pie

Gwen Stice

This recipe was given to me by a dear friend many years ago. At the time, I had never heard of a pear pie, but after trying it for the first time, it became a family favorite.

4 cups pears (peeled, cored, sliced)
1 tbsp butter or margarine
2/3 cup sugar
2 1/2 tsp quick cooking tapioca

1/4 cup lemon juice
1/2 tsp cinnamon
1 unbaked pie shell

Topping:
1/2 cup quick cooking rolled oats
1/3 cup flour
1/3 cup butter or margarine (don't melt)
2 tsp sugar
2 tbsp sliced almonds or walnuts (optional)

In a bowl, blend sliced pears with lemon juice, sugar, cinnamon and tapioca. Let stand for 15 minutes. Pour fruit mixture into an 8 or 9-inch unbaked pie shell and dot with butter. Bake 10 minutes at 375° F. Meanwhile, prepare topping with fork. Sprinkle topping over pie and continue baking 35–40 additional minutes. Makes an 8 or 9 inch pie.

Gwen's Tax & Bookkeeping Service, 131 N. Main Street, Summit, Arkansas, 72677. 870-449-6814 or 870-449-5570 fax. You can E-mail Gwen at gstice@mtnhome.com.

Cookie Tips
* Cookies will spread if your dough is too pliable by allowing butter to get too soft. If your cookies are spreading too much, try refrigerating the dough for a couple of hours before baking.
* Cookie dough can be frozen up to three months in an airtight container or refrigerated three to four days.

Whoopie Pies With Cream Filling

Barbara Linde, Ph.D.

This recipe was a great one for bake sales. I remember eating Whoopie Pies when I was a little girl in Mississippi. The chocolate cookies are good alone without the filling; however, the filling makes them special!

1 cup Crisco (or other) shortening	2 cups sugar
1 egg	1 cup milk
1 tsp vanilla extract	4 cups flour
2 tsp baking powder	2 tsp baking soda
1/2 cup cocoa (dry)	1 tsp salt

Cream Filling:

1 cup shortening (I like Crisco)	1 tsp vanilla extract
1 cup marshmallow cream	1/2 cup milk
1/2 tsp salt	

1 1/2 cups powdered sugar (confectioners sugar)

Cream shortening and sugar; add egg and mix. Mix flour, baking powder, baking soda, dry cocoa and salt in a separate bowl. Add milk and vanilla extract alternately with flour mixture to creamed mixture. Drop by teaspoonfuls on an ungreased cookie sheet. (The size of the cookie will determine the size of the whoopee pie. Try to make all cookies the same size for matching. It takes 2 cookies to make 1 whoopie pie). Bake on an ungreased cookie at 375° F sheet for 10 minutes. Let cookies cool before making your pies. To make cream filling, beat the cream filling ingredients together until fluffy. Spread cream filling on a cookie, top with another cookie to make a "pie".

Peach Betty

Doris Merrill

2 cans sliced peaches (drained)	1/4 stick butter
1 cup graham cracker crumbs	

Place the peaches in an 8x8-inch baking dish. Melt the butter or margarine and mix it evenly into the graham cracker crumbs. Spread the buttered crumbs over the peaches. Bake at 350° F for 30 minutes.

Ozark Blueberry Pie

Carol Landrum

Pie is uniquely American. Our forefathers used what little bits of lard, flour, fruit and buttermilk they had sitting around the house and made something heavenly. I love pie. No one makes good pie anymore. Pie takes time, but it is a labor of love. If you are pressed for time, use a ready made crust. Nothing would tickle me more than having my obituary read, "she could make one hell of a pie!"

1/3 cup flour
2 tbsp butter
1/2 cup sugar (or 1/4 sugar and 1/4 Splenda)
1 tbsp lemon juice
1 pastry for a 9-inch pie (two crust)
1/2 tsp cinnamon (optional but it makes the pie)
4 cup blueberries (or 2 cups blueberries and 2 cups blackberries)

Prepare pastry. Mix sugar, flour and cinnamon. Stir in berries, coating them with sugar and flour mixture. Turn into pastry lined pie plate. Sprinkle with lemon juice and dot with butter. Cover with top crust and make slits for steam to escape. Seal edges and flute. Cover edge with 2-3 inches wide strips of foil (to prevent excess browning of edges during baking). Remove foil during the final 15 minutes of baking. Bake pie at 425° F for 15 minutes and then turn the oven down to 350° F for 20-30 minutes (total baking time will be between 35-45 minutes) or until the crust is brown and juice begins to bubble through the slits.

Apple Crisp

Michella Seawright

8 apples
1 cup flour
1 cup sugar

1/2 tsp salt
1/2 tsp cinnamon
1/2 cup margarine (softened)

Grease an 8x8x2-inch dish. Slice apples into the dish. In another bowl, mix all dry ingredients with margarine and sprinkle over top of apples. Bake at 375 ° F for 45 - 50 minutes.

Buttermilk Coconut Pie

Edith Williams

1 1/2 cups sugar
1 (3 1/2oz) pkg coconut, divided
1 unbaked pastry shell
1/4 cup butter (melted)

1 tsp vanilla extract
3 eggs
1/2 cup buttermilk

Combine sugar and flour. Set aside. Combine eggs and butter, buttermilk and vanilla. Add sugar mixture, stirring well. Stir in 2/3 cup coconut and pour into pie shell. Sprinkle the remaining coconut on top of the pie. Bake at 350° F for 45 minutes.

No Bake Fruit Cake

Dorothy Cotch

My grandmother always made this fruitcake at Christmas time. When I was in grade school she sent the recipe to my mother in a letter, ending the letter with "... hope you like these. Love, love, love and God's blessing."

3/4 cup evaporated milk
1/2 tsp nutmeg
1/2 cup finely cut dates
3 tbsp candied orange peel
6 cups graham cracker crumbs
1/2 cup finely cut candied cherries
1/2 cup finely cut candied pineapple
3 cups midget (mini) marshmallows
1/3 cup orange juice or alcoholic flavoring
1 1/2 cups seeded raisins (1/2 golden & 1/2 dark)

1/2 tsp cinnamon
1/4 tsp ground cloves
1 cup broken walnuts

Grease and line the bottom and sides of a loaf pan with wax paper. Put milk, marshmallows and orange juice into a bowl and mix together. Put all of the other ingredients in a bowl and mix together. Mix in milk mixture with spoon, then with your hands until crumbs are moist. Pack into loaf pan until full. Cover pan with wax paper and weight down with something heavy overnight. It is now ready to tip out of the pan and cut and serve. Makes 1 loaf.

Pear Crisp

Misty Orlove

Cinnamon-spiced pears bake under a crunchy streusel topping in this easy dessert. Assemble the dish ahead of time and put it in the oven when guests arrive. Or bake it earlier in the day and serve it at room temperature. Serve with low-fat vanilla ice cream.

1 1/2 tsp ground cinnamon (divided)
1 tbsp fresh lemon juice   1/3 cup granulated sugar
1/2 cup packed brown sugar   1 tbsp cornstarch
1/3 cup flour (all-purpose)   1/2 tsp salt
1/3 cup oats (not instant)
1/4 cup walnuts (coarsely chopped)
3 tbsp chilled butter (cut into small pieces)
6 cups Anjou or Bartlett pears (cored and cut lengthwise into
    1/2-inch-thick slices, about 3 pounds)

Combine pears and lemon juice in a 2-quart baking dish. Toss gently to coat. Combine granulated sugar, cornstarch and 1 teaspoon cinnamon. Stir with a whisk. Add cornstarch mixture to pear mixture. Toss well to coat. Lightly spoon flour into a dry measuring cup – level with a knife. Place flour, 1/2 teaspoon cinnamon, brown sugar and salt in a food processor. Pulse 2 times or until combined. Add chilled butter. Pulse 6 times or until mixture resembles course meal. Add oats and walnuts. Pulse 2 times. Sprinkle flour mixture evenly over pear mixture. Bake at 375° F for 40 minutes or until pears are tender and topping is golden brown. Cool 20 minutes on a wire rack. Serve warm or at room temperature. Makes 8 servings.

Many fruits and vegetables found in supermarkets today look ripe, but are hard as a rock. Soften them up by placing them in a brown paper bag and hiding the bag away in a dark cabinet for a day or two. This is great for items such as avocados, kiwi fruit, peaches, nectarines, and more. Once ripe, refrigerate the produce to preserve vitamins.

CANDY, DRINKS, SNACKS, THIS & THAT

"Goatville"

Flippin, Arkansas was named for Thomas J. Flippin, who settled in 1821 near where the Marion County Airport is today. However, in the early days, the place was known as Goatville until 1850.

Legend has it that a traveling salesman called on "Uncle Jim Jackson" who had a general store, flour mill and cotton gin. The salesman had not been very successful in selling the 'old goat' any merchandise and started back to his hack in a rather vile mood. To add to his woes one of Mr. Jackson's goats took a running tackle at the seat of his pants, just as he boarded the hack.

Thereafter the enraged salesman's title of "Goatville" stuck. However, the settlers of the now growing community were not happy with the name. So, to honor their first settler, they called the town Flippin Barrens, and eventually the town name was shortened to Flippin.

Flippin General Store

The Ott Family of Flippin

A Lifetime of Love

Howard and Alsey Ott have been happily married for 72 years. They moved to Flippin in 1934 when they married, and have lived here ever since. Today, Alsey is 95 and Howard is 96 years old.

Alsey began cooking at the age of 8 on a wood cook stove when everything had to be made from scratch or you just had to go without. She has seen cooking evolve from her youth when there were no ready-made mixes for anything, to today's grocery stores brimming with convenience foods in every aisle.

When asked what was most special to her about Flippin, Alsey replied, "When we got electric in our home in 1948." Unless you are Alsey and Howard's ages, you can't really appreciate how the world has changed in their lifetime!

Howard and Alsey are special for so many reasons. Alsey served as President of the Flippin Civic Organization for many years, which is a ladies organization. Howard is one of the original workers on the R. M. Ruthven Rainbow Arch Bridge, built in 1930 over the White River in Cotter, Arkansas. He is one of the few workers still living and was honored at the rededication of the bridge in September, 2004. They both have done volunteer work for many organizations, including cooking at the fund raisers,

Howard and Alsey Ott

chili suppers, and fish frys. The couple has always been there to lend a helping hand to families in need during sickness or death.

Howard and Alsey served as Grand Marshals of the Flippin Holi-Dazzle Parade in 2004.

In addition to being an important part of what Flippin is today, Alsey and Howard managed to make time to have two children of their own along the way. Don Ott lives in Lakeview, Arkansas and their daughter Lavon sadly passed away. They have two grandsons and one great grand child.

Below is a wonderful recipe straight from Alsey's own collection. Enjoy!

Yeast Bread   Alsey Ott

4 cups warm water	1 pkg (1 1/2 tbsp) yeast
2 tbsp sugar	1 tbsp salt
1/4 cup shortening	6-6 1/2 cups flour (all purpose)

Dissolve yeast, sugar and salt in water in a large bowl. Add shortening. Gradually mix in flour. Knead on a floured board about 8 minutes. Place in a large greased bowl; turn over once so top of dough is greased. Cover with a towel and allow to rise in a warm place until doubled in bulk (about 1 hour). Punch down. Form dough into 2 loaf pans (greased) for bread or form dough into balls and place in cake pans. Let rise a second time before baking (30–60 minutes). Bake at 375° F until golden brown (approximately 30 minutes).

Butterscotch Surprises

Mary Martin

1 (12 oz) pkg butterscotch morsels
1tbsp peanut butter
1/2 cup broken pecans
1(1 1/2 oz) shoestring potatoes

Melt butterscotch morsels and peanut butter in a pan over boiling water (double boiler). Stir in broken pecans and shoestring potatoes. Drop by teaspoon onto wax paper and allow to cool.

Try to make your candy on dry days. The candy does not set as well on humid or rainy days.

Cocoa Fudge

Sue Pierce

My mother use to make this cooked fudge back in the 40's for our family. I always thought her fudge was the best fudge ever. I make it now for my own family, mostly at Christmas time.

3 cups sugar
1/8 tsp salt
2/3 cup Hershey's cocoa powder
1 can Carnation sweetened condensed milk

1/2 cup butter or margarine
1 tsp pure vanilla

Butter an 8x8-inch square pan and set aside. In a large iron skillet, combine sugar, cocoa and salt. Stir in milk and cook over medium heat, stirring constantly until mixture comes to a full rolling boil. Boil without stirring to 234° F on a candy thermometer (soft ball stage) or when syrup is dropped into cold water and forms a soft ball. Remove from heat. Add vanilla and butter. Beat with a wooden spoon to 110° F and fudge thickens and looses its gloss. Spread into buttered pan and cool. Makes 3 dozen pieces.

Peanut Brittle

Myrt Flippin

1 cup sugar	1 tsp baking soda
1 cup light corn syrup	2 cups raw peanuts
1 tsp vanilla extract	2 tbsp butter
1/4 cup water	

Combine sugar, syrup and 1/4 cup of water in a saucepan. Cook to soft ball stage (approximately 240° F on a candy thermometer). Add peanuts. Cook until light brown in color. Add vanilla and butter, stirring to blend. Add baking soda and stir briskly until thoroughly dissolved. Pour onto foil-lined baking sheet. Cool, break into pieces.

Pralines

Anne Presley

This recipe won my sister Sue first place in the candy category of the 1984 Frankfort Kentucky United Way Bake Off. Growing up in Louisiana, pralines were always a favorite. Sue gave the recipe to my sister Maureen who started making them for Holiday gatherings. My sister Julia and I have made them for other occasions. However, for family get-togethers, we rely on Maureen for her tradition.

1 1/2 cups sugar	1 tsp vanilla extract
1 1/2 cups brown sugar	1/4 tsp cream of tarter
1 cup milk or half & half	1/2 tsp salt
1/4 cup butter or margarine	
2 1/2 cups pecan (halves or pieces)	

Bring sugar, brown sugar, salt, milk and cream of tarter to a boil. Stir over low heat until sugar dissolves. Continue to cook to a soft ball stage 238° F. Turn off heat. Cool to 220° F. Add butter, vanilla and pecans. Beat until creamy with a wire whisk. Drop by spoonful onto buttered waxed paper or buttered foil.

Optional: For maple sugar pralines substitute maple syrup for brown sugar or use maple extract instead of vanilla.

Easy Chocolate Truffles

Lois Drake

The original recipe calls for orange flavoring, but you can use many other variations such as: lemon flavoring and lemon zest, raspberry flavoring (6 tablespoons raspberry liquor), coffee flavor using 6 tablespoons of Kailua, pineapple flavoring and roll in chopped coconut, add nuts to chocolate mixture, roll truffles in crushed nuts, roll truffles in candy sprinkles... the possibilities are endless, just use your imagination!

1 pkg (8oz) semi-sweet chocolate chips (3/4 of a 12 oz bag)
1 stick butter, salted or unsalted (I use salted)
1 (14 oz) can sweetened condensed milk
2 tsp orange extract flavoring
   zest of 1 good-sized orange
4 oz unsweetened chocolate (chopped up)
   (or I use 4 packets Nestle Choco-Bake, it's simplest)
1 pkg almond bark

Heat chocolate, butter and milk until partially melted. Remove from heat and stir until all is melted. Stir or whisk in orange flavoring and zest. Transfer mixture to bowl and let stand until firm enough to hold its shape (about 2–2 1/2 hours). Scoop small amount into your hand and roll into balls, about 1 inch in size. Place truffles on a cookie sheet on waxed paper. Refrigerate until firm (this makes them easier to handle). Melt dark (or white) almond bark and thin to a good coating consistency. (Follow directions on the package for thinning the chocolate). With a toothpick or thin skewer, pierce the hardened balls and dip in the almond bark. Gently shake off excess coating. Slide ball off with another pick onto waxed paper and allow to set. You can "fix" the hole from the pick with a little melted coating dabbed on with the pick. Store in refrigerator. Before serving, let stand at room temperature to soften slightly.

Fudge
Jo Ann Huddleston Roden

3 cups sugar
1/4 tsp salt
4 tbsp butter

2/3 cup cocoa (almost)
1 2/3 cup milk
1 1/2 tsp vanilla extract

Stir together dry ingredients well. Add milk. Heat on medium-high heat stirring constantly until it begins to boil – then stop stirring immediately and do not stir again. Here's the tricky part: to determine when the fudge has boiled long enough, drop some off of a spoon into a glass of cold water. When the droppings no longer break apart and can be rolled together easily, remove from heat. Add butter and vanilla. Cool approximately 15 minutes and beat the fudge vigorously. Drop the fudge from a spoon onto wax paper.

Note: If the fudge doesn't harden, it was under cooked.

Jo Ann Huddleston Roden is the granddaughter of Ida And William Treat.

Granola Fudge Butterscotch Clusters
Ina Johnson

These are yummy, fast and need no baking!

1 cup chocolate chips
1 cup butterscotch chips
1 1/4 cups granola (without raisins)
1 cup chopped walnuts

Melt together chocolate chips and butterscotch chips. Add granola and nuts, mix well. Drop by spoonfuls onto wax paper. Chill 30-45 minutes, until set.

Old-Time Grape Nuts Pudding
Phyllis Hoy

I loved custard and have tried to use a cereal with it. In those days, everyone was using cereal in their recipes in order to expand the servings and for a different flavor.

1/4 cup butter	1/8 tsp salt
3/4 cup Grape Nuts cereal	1 tsp vanilla extract
3 eggs	2 cups milk
1/2 cup sugar	

In an 8-inch skillet over low heat, melt butter. Remove from heat, stir in Grape Nuts; set aside. In a mixing bowl, beat eggs until thickened; gradually beat in sugar, milk, salt and vanilla. Stir in Grape Nuts mixture. Pour into 6, 6-ounce glass custard cups. Place in a shallow pan of hot water halfway up the custard cups. Bake in a preheated 375° F oven for 20 minutes, stirring twice at 10 minute intervals, then bake without stirring 15 minutes longer until a silver knife inserted in center comes out clean. Chill. Serve with whipped topping. Makes 6 servings.

Peanut Brittle
Elsie Treat Wood Keith

This was also a favorite recipe of Ruby Treat Williams

1 cup sugar	1/2 cup water
1/2 cup white corn syrup	1 cup peanuts (shelled)
1 tbsp butter	1 tbsp vanilla extract

Mix sugar, water and corn syrup in a sauce pan and bring to a boil. Continue to boil to the "thread stage" (until they spin a thread when poured off a spoon). Add peanuts to hot liquid and continue cooking until peanuts have all popped. Add butter and vanilla. Pour hot liquid onto buttered cookie sheet. Cool and break into pieces.

Elsie Treat Wood Keith is the daughter of Ida And William Treat.

Hot Chocolate Mix
Jane Herbst

1 (8 qt) box powdered milk
1 (6 oz) jar of Coffee-Mate
2 lb can Nestlé's Quick or similar

1–2 cups powdered sugar
pinch of salt

Mix all dry ingredients together until well mixed. Store in a tightly-covered container. To serve, mix with boiling water, about 3 rounded tablespoons in a mug.

Hot Mulled Cider
Edith Williams

1 gallon apple cider
1 tsp ground allspice
1 tsp whole cloves

2 cups brown sugar
1 tsp cinnamon
orange slices for garnish

Mix apple cider with brown sugar. Combine allspice, cinnamon and whole cloves into a square of cheesecloth and tie tightly. Add this packet to the cider mixture. Heat to a boil, reduce heat and simmer for 10 minutes. Serve in mugs garnished with orange slices. Refrigerate any leftovers and reheat as desired.

Red Hot Cinnamon Cider
Jane Herbst

1 quart apple cider (4 cups)
1/4 cup red hot cinnamon candies

Combine cider and candies in a saucepan. Bring to a boil and simmer until candies dissolve. Garnish with a cinnamon stick stirrer, if desired. Makes 8, 1/2 cup servings.

Sherbet Punch
Jane Herbst

1/2 gallon Sherbet

2 1/2 qts 7-up (very cold)

Put sherbet in a punch bowl and gently pour in the 7-UP. Serving size: 5 oz cup, quantity 50.

Instant Hot Cocoa

Martha Berkshire Buchs

We use this basic recipe for the cocoa we serve after the annual Flippin Holi-Dazzle Christmas Parade. As an Air Force wife, this was a favorite hot drink mix for many families. Adding the optional malted milk powder makes your hot cocoa richer and even more delicious.

1 lb powdered milk
1 lb Nesquick powder
1 lb powdered creamer
1 lb malted milk powder (optional)
1 lb powdered sugar
miniature marshmallows (optional)

Blend ingredients well. Store in an air tight container. Use 1/4 cup of mixture in an 8 oz cup. Add hot water and stir until dissolved. Top with miniature marshmallows. Enjoy!

Spiced Tea

Michella Seawright

2 1/3 cups sugar	1 pkg Wyler's lemonade mix
3/4 cup instant tea	1/2 tsp cinnamon
1 1/2 cups Tang	1/2 tsp cloves

Mix well and store in dry place. To make tea; stir 2 teaspoons of spiced tea mixture into hot water in a cup.

Bacon BBQ Water Chestnuts
Michella Seawright

whole water chestnuts
toothpicks
bacon

Sauce:
1 cup ketchup
3/4 cup sugar
dash of soy sauce or cooking sherry
1/4 cup brown sugar
dash of Worcestershire sauce

Wrap each chestnut with 1/2 slice bacon and secure with toothpicks. Bake at 350° F for 30 minutes. Drain. Combine remaining ingredients; pour over bacon wrapped chestnuts. Return to 350° F oven for 30 additional minutes.

Bread Boat
Sherry Berthot

This recipe was given to me by a former co-worker. We always enjoyed having this on special occasions at work.

1 (12 oz) pkg Carl Budding chopped corn beef
2 tsp Beau Monde Seasoning   **2 tsp dill weed**
1 1/3 cups sour cream   **1 loaf rye bread**
2 tsp onion powder   **1 1/2 cups mayonnaise**

Mix ingredients together and chill. Cut top off the rye bread. Then carve out the inside. Cut removed bread into cubes and store in a plastic bag. When ready to serve, put filling into bread boat. Use pieces of bread for dipping!

Seven Layer Mexi-Dip

Gail Major

This recipe has been used by my family for years. It is a common recipe used by many. I just add the jalapeño peppers because that is what we like. You can layer as you like. Best served with "Scoops".

1 can bean dip
1 small can black olives (chopped)
1 small tomato   3 green onions (chopped)
1 (8 oz) pkg sour cream   1 (6 oz) pkg shredded cheese
1/2 pkg taco seasoning   jalapeño peppers (optional)
1 (8 oz) can guacamole dip

Layer bean dip followed by guacamole dip. Combine sour cream and taco seasoning packet together for the next layer. Layer tomatoes, black olives, green onions and shredded cheese. Chill for at least 2 hours. Serve with chips or "Scoops".

Optional: You can use fat free ingredients to lower the calories. If you like a spicy dip, add jalapeño peppers on top.

French Dip Venison Sandwiches

Sandy Garrison

This recipe is one that is great to throw in the crock-pot before I leave for work in the morning.

1 venison ham roast   3 cups water
1 pkg brown gravy mix   2 tbsp black pepper
1 tsp salt   2 bell peppers (optional)
1 medium onion (optional)   1 pkg hoagie rolls
1 pkg of McCormick Au Jus mix
2 tbsp olive oil (optional with peppers and onion)

Place venison roast in crock-pot with water, salt, pepper and add brown gravy mix. Cook on high for 6-8 hours. Drain roast and slice against the grain. Sauté green peppers and onion in olive oil. Toast buns. Prepare Au Jus as directed for dipping. Layer sliced venison, onion and peppers on rolls. Serve each sandwich with Au Jus on the side for dipping.

Spicy Walnuts
Pamelia Senger

I found this recipe in an old cookbook. I've been making them for over 40 years. They are great as a holiday gift!

2 1/2 cups walnuts	1 1/2 tsp vanilla extract
1 cup granulated sugar	1/2 cup water
1 tsp cinnamon	1/2 tsp salt

Heat walnut halves in pan at 375° F for 5 minutes, stirring once. Butter sides of a 2-quart sauce pan. In it combine sugar, water, cinnamon and salt. Cook and stir until sugar dissolves and mixture boils. Cook without stirring to the soft ball stage (236° F on a candy thermometer). Remove from heat. Beat by hand for 1 minute or until the mixture just begins to get creamy. Add vanilla and warm nuts; stir gently until nuts are well coated and mixture is creamy. Turn out on a buttered platter or cookie sheet Separate at once, using 2 forks. Makes about 1 pound.

Spinach Tortilla Rolls
Ina Johnson

1/4 cup mayonnaise
1/4 cup bacon (crumbled)
6 green onions (chopped)
2 (10 oz) pkg frozen, chopped spinach
1 pkg Hidden Valley Ranch dressing mix
2 (8 oz) pkg cream cheese (softened)
7 large flour tortillas (soft taco or burrito size)

Ahead of time, thaw spinach and squeeze out water. Beat together softened cream cheese and mayonnaise. Add dressing mix, bacon bits and onion; blend well. Mix in spinach. Spread mix on tortillas to edges. Roll up. Cover with plastic wrap and refrigerate for 6 hours or overnight. Before serving, slice into 1-inch pinwheels. Discard "dead" space on the ends of the tortillas. Arrange on serving plate. Chill and serve. Makes 7 burrito-sized tortillas.

Bacon Swiss Bread

Judy Martin

1 loaf french bread
8 oz swiss cheese slices
1/3 cup chopped green onions
1 tbsp mustard

1 tbsp poppy seeds
1/2 cup butter (softened)
4–5 slices bacon strips

Cut bread into 1 inch thick slices, leaving slices attached at the bottom. Cut each slice of cheese diagonally and place triangle of cheese between each slice of bread. Place loaf on foil-covered cookie sheet. Combine butter, onion, mustard and poppy seeds, mixing well. "Ice" bread on top and side with butter/mustard mixture. Place small pieces of bacon on top. Bake at 400° F for 20– 25 minutes or until bacon is crisp. Serve hot.

Dried Beef Dip

Jane Herbst

1 (8 oz) pkg cream cheese
1 (3-4oz) pkg dried beef

1 (8 oz) carton sour cream
garlic and onion salt to taste

Mix ingredients well and refrigerate.

Chocolate Gravy

Kail Wilkes

1/2 stick butter
4 tbsp flour
2 cups milk

3 tbsp cocoa
3/4 cup sugar
1 1/2 tsp vanilla extract

Mix cocoa, flour and sugar; add butter and milk. Cook over medium heat until thick. Serve over hot biscuits.

Oyster Cracker Snacks
Jane Herbst

1 scant cup of oil
1/2 tsp garlic
1 pkg Hidden Valley Dressing (dry)

1 1/2 tsp dill
1 pkg oyster crackers

Heat oil until hot. Add other ingredients. Pour over oyster crackers and stir or shake until coated.

Maui Artichoke and Crab Dip
Lynne Moore

3/4 tsp cayenne pepper
1/3 cup Dijon mustard
12 oz cooked crab meat
2 (16 oz) loaves King's Hawaiian sweet bread
1 cup mayonnaise (I use Miracle Whip)
1 can artichoke hearts (drained and chopped)
8 oz shredded cheddar cheese (divided)

3 (8 oz) pkg cream cheese
1 tsp garlic powder

Slice a thin layer from the top of the loaf of bread. Carefully hollow out the loaf leaving 1 inch on sides and bottom. Cube removed bread and cube an additional loaf. Mix remainder of ingredients, except cheddar cheese. Warm the mixture in microwave or on top of stove. Mix 1/2 of the cheddar cheese with warmed mixture and then pour into hollowed out loaf. Garnish with remaining cheese. Arrange bread cubes around loaf of dip when ready to serve. Serve warm or cold.

Fresh Homemade Salsa
Pam Hurst

3 medium tomatoes
1/4 cup onion (chopped)
2 medium jalapeno peppers (chopped)

2 tbsp white wine vinegar
1 tsp salt

Combine all ingredients and stir well. Let stand at room temperature for about 30 minutes before serving. Store leftovers in refrigerator. Makes 3 cups.

Spinach Dip

Joanne Berger

I had this dip at a party over 35 years ago. A number of guests wouldn't try it because of the spinach. So, when I served it, I never told anyone that it was spinach until AFTER they tasted it and remarked how good it was. Several said they didn't like spinach but loved the dip!

1/2 tsp pepper	2 cups mayonnaise
1/2 cup dried parsley	1/2 cup green onions (chopped)
1 scant tsp salt	
1 pkg chopped frozen spinach (thaw and drain)	

Thaw spinach and drain. Mix all ingredients and chill overnight. Serve with raw vegetables or crackers.

> Steak Sauce With A Kick: Deglaze your frying pan (after searing your New York steaks) with brandy. Add two tablespoons of butter, a little white wine and a splash of Grand Marnier. Serve over steaks - you'll never use steak sauce again.

Hamburger Sauce

Brenda Young

I usually double this recipe and use the sauce as gravy for mashed potatoes.

1/2 cup ketchup	onion to taste
1/2 cup water	3 tbsp sugar
1 tbsp vinegar	1 tbsp Worcestershire sauce

Mix ingredients in a sauce pan. Pour over fried hamburger patties. Bake at 350° F for 20 minutes.

> Professionally decorated cakes have a silky, molten look. To get that appearance, frost your cake as usual, then use a hair dryer to blow-dry the surface until the frosting slightly melts.

Chocolate Mint Frosting

Rita Ross

Use this frosting for brownies!

5 tbsp milk
3/4 tsp vanilla extract
6 tbsp unsalted butter (softened)
2 cups sifted confectioners' sugar
1/4 cup chopped fresh chocolate mint
2 1/2 oz unsweetened chocolate, melted

In small mixer bowl, cream butter at medium speed of electric mixer. Gradually add 2 cups confectioners' sugar, beating well after each addition. Add 3/4 tsp vanilla extract in melted unsweetened chocolate. Beat until smooth. Gradually add remaining 1 cup confectioners' sugar with cooled milk, beating until smooth. After each addition, continue to beat until frosting is creamy and spreading consistency. Spread frosting on cooled brownies. Cut in squares and serve.

Beat and Eat Frosting

Dorothy Schill

3/4 cup of sugar	1/4 teaspoon of cream of tarter
1 tsp vanilla extract	1/4 cup boiling water
1 egg white	

Place egg white and cream of tarter, vanilla and sugar in large bowl, a bowl that an electric mixer will fit. Mix and beat until stands on peaks. This will ice 1 large sheet cake or 2 layers.

One Minute Chocolate Frosting

Dorothy Schill

1 stick of melted butter	1 cup of sugar
1/4 cup of cocoa	1/4 cup of milk

Cook over low heat and be sure the sugar melts. Boil 1 minute. Cool slightly and beat until thick.

Grape "Ketchup" Lois Drake

This is rather labor intensive but if you ever taste it over pork chops or fried potatoes and onions, you'll never eat them again without this "ketchup". This is a recipe that my grandma (born 1882) had... don't know how old it really is. I grew up with it. It keeps forever. I guess it's called Ketchup because of its consistency. Nice deep purple color when fresh... but even if it's years old and turns brown, it tastes just as good (probably even better) and won't kill 'ya. At least I'm still around to tell the tale!!!

1 tbsp cinnamon	1/2 tbsp salt
1 tbsp ground cloves	1 tbsp allspice

5 lb purple grapes (concord is best)
1/2 cup + 2 lb light brown sugar
1 tbsp ground black pepper
1 pint cider vinegar (not white)

Squeeze (squooch) the grapes out of their skins with your fingers. Cook grapes and skins together in at least a 5-quart pot, until kinda mushy-soft. Put mixture into a coarse sieve a little at a time and stir it around with the back of a spoon to push as much pulp and skin through as possible. Discard seeds and repeat until all cooked grapes and skins have been strained to a pulp/juice mix. Add remaining ingredients. Boil until thick (about the consistency of "cheap" ketchup). Seal, using proper canning method, into jelly jars and cool.

Note: Use no less than a 5-quart pot. Non-stick is best. Grape juice has a tendency to "expand" when cooked, so watch your heat so it doesn't boil over.

> Ground spices really should be replaced every 6 months or so! Unless you know you will use them up fairly quickly, buy a bottle in partnership with a friend and split the contents. You'll each benefit from fresh spices.

Cold Vegetable Pizza   Sharon Foster

This recipe is from an elderly lady that I used to work with. She had brought it one time when we had a party at work. It was really good and you didn't have to worry about heating it up.

2 carrots (shredded)   4 cauliflowerettes
1 (8 oz) pkg cream cheese   1 cup Miracle Whip (light)
2 stalks broccoli (tops only) 1/2 green pepper (chopped)
1 green onion (chopped)
1 envelope reduced calorie ranch dressing
2 (8 oz) cans Pillsbury crescent rolls
8 oz shredded cheese – mozzarella,
    cheddar Monterey jack or a mixture.

Unroll crescent rolls and press edges together on a cookie sheet Bake at 375° F for 10 minutes. Cool crust. Mix cream cheese, ranch dressing and miracle whip. Spread on cooled crust. Chop all vegetables finely, sprinkle on top of your pizza. Top with shredded cheese. Cut like pizza. Serve cold.

French Bread Baking Tips
Use an egg wash to make the crust really brown up. French bread must have a high temperature to bake properly. Check your oven to make sure the temperature is correct. Add a little sugar to the mix to help brown up your crust.

Cheesy French Bread   Mrs. John (Tootsie) Sonntag

This recipe came from "Sivils" family cookbook – Very Good!

1 cup mayonnaise
1 stick butter or oleo (softened)
1 (4oz) can chopped green chilies (drained)
1 loaf French bread (split lengthwise)
1 1/2 cups monterey jack cheese with pepper (grated)

Combine all ingredients and spread on both halves of French bread loaf. Bake at 400° F until bubbly and browned.

Advertisers:
Thank you for your support!
the Flippin Pride Team

453-HAIR
453-4247

Owner   Stylist
Vicki BiLyeu

CUTTING EDGE
"Men & Women's Hair Cutting"

401 HWY. 62
FLIPPIN, AR

Cabins   **Boats**

L.C.

On Bull Shoals Lake

Richard & Joyce Keller
790 CR 505
Mountain Home, AR 72653
1-870-431-5561
toll free: 1-877-269-2729
e-mail: battysresort@centurytel.net
www.battysresort.com

Your Trout Fishing Destination
White Hole Resort
Free Fishing Information!

Clean & Comfortable Cabins
Courteous Fishing Guides
Reliable Boat Rentals
Delicious Meal Services

Crystal Clear River
Rugged Bluffs
Bait, Spin or Fly Fishing
Family Friendly

Operated with Christian Family Values
White Hole Resort
www.WhiteHoleResort.com   *toll-free: 1-866-781-6056*
Flippin, Arkansas

FLIPPIN
Chamber of Commerce

Flippin Area Chamber of Commerce
P.O. Box 118
Flippin, AR 72634
(870) 453-8480
www.flippinchamber.com

Flippin is located in the beautiful Ozark mountains of North Central Arkansas. Fishing and boating highlight Flippin's way of life situated close to Bull Shoals Lake, the famous White River and the Buffalo National River and Park.

Flippin has excellent schools, access to nearby higher educational institutions, scenic beauty, pleasantly mild climate, access to high quality medical care, safe environment, and outstanding recreational opportunities along with friendly residents to round out the Flippin lifestyle.

"The Home of Ranger Boats"

Flippin is known as the home of "Ranger" bass boats, a vital industry in the Flippin area. A considerable number of residents work in the tourism industry. Other industries include molded plastics and cable technology. There are two industrial parks with over 100 acres available inside the city limits.

Come, and visit Flippin!

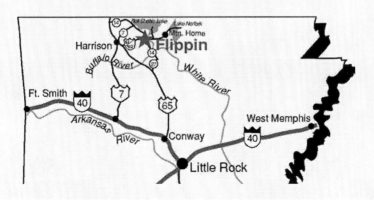

STILL BUILDING
LEGENDS...
ONE AT A TIME

Experience the only genuine Best Built-Best Backed boats in America.
See your local Ranger dealer and find out how easy it is to run the rig of your dreams.

For The Name
Of Your Nearest Ranger Dealer, Call:
1-800-373-BOAT (2628)

Will special order any leather item!
Layaways welcome!
We accept Visa/MC

Hog Heaven Leather & Gifts

Jim & Bonnie Tudor
P.O. Box 1216
209 East Main Street

Motorcycle Jackets, Chaps, Vests & Accessories
Dress & Casual Leather

Flippin, AR

870-453-5194

EXIT AL PAGE REALTY

Al Page, Broker
office: (870) 424-5512
toll free: (800)-424-6880

AL & Gunner
Mountain Home, Arkansas

+TANNING
+EXERCISE
+BODY WRAPS

FROG WILD

P.O. Box 1779
503 E. Main Street
Flippin, AR 72634

453-FROG (3764)

Flippin
203 E. Main Street
Flippin, AR 72634
(870) 453-RENT

BEST RENTAL
Rent To Own
Furniture & Appliances

Mountain Home
1322 Hiway 62 East
Mountain Home, AR 72653
(870) 425-2397

Phone: (870) 435-6181
Fax: (870) 435-6184
Toll Free: (888)-308-6181
Home: (870) 425-5655
6703 Hiway 62 West, Gassville, AR 72635
E-mail: cherokee @mtnhome.com

CHEROKEE REALTY

ILENE STEVENSON
Life Member
Million $ Club

MLS

OAK GROVE RV PARK

THE SHADY PLACE TO CAMP

A Branson Favorite for 50 Years!

Shady Oak Trees	Picnic tables
Open Year Round	Benches & Grills
Beautiful Views	Full hook-up Service
Close to Attractions	Laundry Room
Lakes / Dams	Cable TV

George & Sharla Shivers
General Managers

780 State Highway 165
Branson, MO 65616
phone: 417-334-4781
toll free: 888-334-4781
cell: 417-593-1235
fax: 417-239-0424
e-mail: oakgrovervpark@yahoo.com
www.oakgrovervpark.com

To receive a discount on a show ticket purchase, just say:
"I found Oak Grove RV Park in the Flippin Pride Team Cookbook!"

BRANSON SHENANIGANS R.V. PARK

WALK TO BRANSON SHOWS!

12 theaters, outlet shopping, restaurants and attractions... all within a 3 to 20 minute walk. (Or take the shuttle for a small fee.)

- Full Hookups • Pull-Thru Spaces
- 30/50 Amps • Clubhouse • Laundry
- Tree Shaded Sites • Free Cable TV
- Private, Sparkling Clean Bathrooms
- Show Reservation Assistance Upon Your Arrival

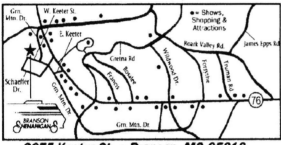

"We've been through every state but two... this is the nicest campground we've ever been in!"

MENTION THIS AD AND RECEIVE

$3.00 OFF

FIRST NIGHT

3675 Keeter St. • Branson, MO 65616
www.bransonrvparks.com • bsrvpark@aol.com
For Resv: *Call (800) 338-7275* • For Info: *Call (417) 334-1920*

OPEN EARLY, OPEN LATE

Have a particular time you like to do your banking? With Arvest Bank, we give you more options than anyone else. Convenient branch locations open from 7 to 7 are here to serve you, making your day easier. Live life on your schedule, that's why we're here – Arvest Bank.

(870) 453-5626

Here when you need us.

arvest.com

Member FDIC

137

White River
Famous Floats

"We have been planning your float trip since 1966!"

870-453-4918
Toll Free **1-888-538-9896**

1409 Hwy 178 • Bull Shoals, AR 72619

www.famousfloats.com or
http://whiteriver.net/famousfloats

Flippin Family Practice

Roger Simons M.D.

111 E. Main Place #3
P.O. Box 550
Flippin, AR 72634
(870) 453-2274

PUSH, PULL, PLOW, HAUL, TOW, SCRAPE...

We have everything you need to make your hard-working Polaris ATV work even harder.

POLARIS®
RIDE THE BEST

Polaris of the Ozarks
Flippin, AR
870-453-2382

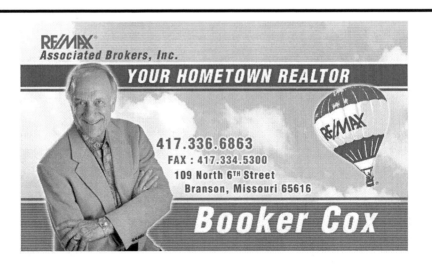

RE/MAX®
Associated Brokers, Inc.

YOUR HOMETOWN REALTOR

417.336.6863
FAX : 417.334.5300
109 North 6TH Street
Branson, Missouri 65616

Booker Cox

MyHotSauces.Com L.L.C.
Award Winning
Sauces For Every Type
Of Chilihead!

Visit Us On The Web At:
www.MyHotSauces.Com

North Arkansas
Abstract & Title Company

Title Insurance
Escrow Services
Real Estate Closings

Licensed Title Agents & Abstracters

Dick Wendel - President
Lois Stonecipher
Gina Baker
David Drake - Closing Agent

Licensed Title Agent
Crystal Powell

870-449-4207

fax: 870-449-5724
307 E. Old Main
P.O. Box 250
Yellville, AR 72687

RECIPE FOR SUCCESS

1 lb	Cheerfulness
1 1/3	cup Helpfulness
1 1/3	cup Courtesy
1	tbsp Confidence
3	tbsp Respect
1	Pinch of Perseverance
1	Good Measure of Loyalty

Topping:

2	cups Integrity
3	cups Experience
21	tbsp Teamwork

1. Combine 1 lb Cheerfulness and 1 1/3 cup of Helpfulness, and cook over medium heat until boiling.

2. Mix together 1 1/3 cup Courtesy, 1 tbsp Confidence and 3 tbsp of Respect until well blended.

3. Add a Pinch of Perseverance, good measure of Loyalty and season to taste. Blend with Cheerfulness, Helpfulness, Courtesy, Confidence and Respect and pour into pan and bake at 365 until well done.

4. For topping, mix together 2 cups Integrity, 3 cups Experience and 21 tbsp of Teamwork. Remove pie from oven and sprinkle topping over warm pie.

5. Enjoy!

Larry Black
& Associates, Inc.
Real Estate

River And Lake Homes • Acreage
Commercial • Land Development

425-9898

142

Recipe Index

Recipe Index

Candy, Drinks, Snacks, This n' That

Cookbook Authors

Cookbook Authors

Flippin Good Recipes,
From Flippin Arkansas

What a great gift-giving idea for all the history buffs, cooks, hunters or friends and family members that you want to present with a cookbook that is not only humorous but is also brimming with great recipes and so much more! Order enough copies to cover all your gift-giving needs this year.

Be sure to watch our website for Volume 2 which has even more great recipes that will fill your belly and great stories that will warm your heart and make you smile!

Qty
ordered   **Total**

_____ Flippin Good Recipes, Vol 1 $12.95 (US Funds) _____
        ISBN# 0-9772372-3-0
Shipping & Handling   _____
(add $3.00 for first book and $1.00 for each additional book)
Order Total   _____

Ship To:
Name: _____

Address: _____

_____

City/State:_____
Zip: _____
Phone: _____
E-mail address: _____

For credit card orders, call our toll free line at **800-700-5096** or visit our website at **flippinprideteam.org.**
Mail your order form to: The Flippin Pride Team, P.O. Box 1191, Flippin, AR 72634. All mail orders are shipped via media mail, please allow 2 - 4 weeks for delivery. For faster delivery, call our 800# or visit us on the web!